Courage

The Heart and Spirit of Every Woman

Courage

The Heart and Spirit of Every Woman

Reclaiming the Forgotten Virtue

SANDRA FORD WALSTON

Broadway Books
New York

BROADWAY

Broadway Books titles may be purchased for business or promotional use or for special sales. For information, please write to: Special Markets Department, Random House, Inc., 1540 Broadway, New York, NY 10036.

BROADWAY BOOKS and its logo, a letter B bisected on the diagonal, are trademarks of Broadway Books, a division of Random House, Inc.

Visit our website at www.broadwaybooks.com

Library of Congress Cataloging-in-Publication Data
Walston, Sandra Ford, 1946–
   Courage: the heart and spirit of every woman : reclaiming the forgotten virtue / Sandra Ford Walston.—1st ed.
      p. cm.
   Includes bibliographical references and index.
   1. Courage. 2. Women—Psychology. I. Title.

BF575.C8 W35 2001
179'.6'082—dc21   00-066721

FIRST EDITION

Designed by Diane Hobbing of Snap-Haus Graphics

FOOTPRINTS IN THE SAND by Mary Stevenson with permission by Kathy M. Hampton AKA Kathy Bee

ISBN 0-7679-0762-0
10 9 8 7 6 5 4 3 2 1

Dedicated to
David.
Always loved,
Never forgotten.

CONTENTS

Part Two

Part Four

Contents

Special Acknowledgments to the Courageous Women

This page acknowledges the women who assisted me in researching and writing this book. They graciously contributed their precious time and honored me with their life's stories. Most of the interviewees and I cried during the interview process as each personal anecdote revealed the stations of courage in their lives. Their passages exemplified every woman.

For over three years while I fumbled on my courageous journey, the women who responded to the survey form and qualified to be interviewed as "courageous women" offered support and love. I am sad to write that I lost touch with a few of them; nevertheless, all of the women gave their heart and spirit. Their names are listed on the next page based on their personal request. Some use their actual name, some use their first name only, and some use a fictitious name. I am honored to acknowledge them, and I thank them from the core of my being for joining spirits on this courageous journey.

Alexis Ralston

Angela

Anne

Ava Simmons

Bonnie Barnes

Candace

Carol Francis Rinehart

Carol Veatch

Cene Backus

Corinne

Danielle

Debra Heskin

Diane

Donna Baumer

Eva Ortiz

Goldie Cohn

Jan

Jennifer

Joan Badzik

Jody

Karen McGee

Kay

Laurie Graves

Lila

Linda Betz

Louise

Louise D.

Lynda

Lynette Horan

Lynn Fullerton

M. Hayes

Maria G.

Mary

Michelle Gaschler

Murph Super

Myrna Benoit

Rebecca

Roberta Monaco

Ruthie

Sarah Thompson

Sally J. Kelly

Sheryl

Sheryl Luttringer

Stephie Allen

Stephanie

Sue Pierce

Susan M. Davis

Theresa Hart-Kanan

Tracy Hawn

Tracy Jenkins

Virginia Heidinger

PERSONAL ACKNOWLEDGMENTS

Finally, the time has arrived to personally acknowledge everyone who helped me bring this book to fruition. What a joy to thank the gracious souls who supported my heart's passion. Few people knew many years ago that I wanted to write a book on women and courage. The concept remained tucked away in my mind until the time finally arrived to discover if my vision had validity.

Ironically, it could not begin to materialize until I owned a computer. In December 1994 my mother generously gave me the money to buy my first laptop, and I started randomly collecting my ideas and gathering materials with the thought that one day I would actually start the book. In March 1995, I took a class in goal setting, which had us outline in detail five specific areas of our life that we wanted to convert into reality. In my career section, I listed "writing a nonfiction book on women and courage" as the primary goal I wanted to achieve in the next five years. To define this goal, I wrote very specific action steps in the order of their importance and listed eight tasks that I needed to accomplish.

Asked to check off items under the heading "required improvement to succeed," I instinctively checked off only one item: "the ability to live with uncertainty." I had not yet learned to live with uncertainty. Little did I realize how much my faith would be challenged during the project, and how difficult it would be to remain hopeful throughout the journey. The ability to live with uncertainty was key.

I had no idea how to start the process of writing

a book. I met Mary Cook, an author and human resources consultant. She told me I had a great idea and that I should write about my concept. She became a friend and mentor.

Janet Long taught me how to utilize my software applications, and for more than two years she spent weeks transcribing my interviews. Karen Gilleland also encouraged me to continue writing.

I am blessed with extremely gifted and devoted women friends, who each rallied around me. My dear friend, Lauren Hildebrand, edited my initial, poorly written work that revealed my fear to move from my intellectual head to my vulnerable heart. Living out of state, she always responded quickly to edit my faxes, many times neglecting her own work to help me. She provided positive support and never left me hanging, including editing the very last chapter. Last, but not least, she provided the inspiration and artistic elements for the original book cover and the symbol representing heart and spirit.

When Catharyn Baird and I met at a dinner party, I immediately knew I was at the gathering to meet this special woman. I even said, "Who are you? I must get to know you." We found we had much in common, and she quickly became a valued friend. About every ten days for more than a year, Catharyn came to my condo, made her way to the patio table in my dining room, stepping over papers and books strewn all over the floor, and provided me with emotional courage. Sitting shoulder to shoulder, she was my security blanket. She guided me through setbacks, frustrations, and hurts until I grew to find the voice of my own message and the hidden writer within.

Every time uncertainty reared its scary head, a

friend showed up to brainstorm my thesis or edit. One day my precious friend, Angelique Matney, and I met at a sidewalk coffee café. As we visited, I found myself struggling to find my voice and clarity in the book's message. Pretending to be Oprah, Angelique asked me questions that helped me to clarify the meaning. Each insight narrowed the heart of the idea. Struggles and fears in the form of sparse income, depression, and discouragement threatened to stop me. But each time, God sent me a helper—what I call "reaching hands"—someone to offer their gifts and their support. Reverend Analea Rawson, Senior Pastor for The Christ Way CommUNITY Church, inspired me to live my faith.

I met Becky Lennon when I did a presentation to a professional women's group she belonged to and I mentioned my book on women and courage. After the program I told her, "As a potential buyer of my book, you may be what I call a tough customer because you enjoy a book with substance and concrete evidence. Would you consider reading my book?" Becky, a lawyer and writer in her own right, talented and caring, agreed to read it. Busy with a new baby and a hectic schedule, she not only read but also edited my entire draft and galley. What a blessing to have her input and new-found friendship.

Anne Lieberman cheered me up more than once. And Tom Kanan took time away from his busy life and law practice to put on his "Professor of English" hat to edit several proposals. Dee Marvine edited the manuscript. I'm sure I drove her nuts at times. She contributed unique gifts each step of the way. Additionally, a special "thank you" to the librarians at Ross–University Hills Branch Library for all their support with my research, and for their patience while I invaded the corner conference room for many long years to conduct my interviews.

Once the complete manuscript was in the first rounds of edit, I met another talented woman at an Enneagram class, Anne Stanwick. I was touched when she not only offered to read my book but said that she would be honored to help me with marketing. I wanted to cry—the privilege of having her expertise was mine. At the end of the journey other gifted women appeared—Carolyn Seigneur and Ann Marie Gordon. With each set of eyes, my "baby" became more refined, and I became more certain that my calling was indeed becoming a reality.

There were many times during these years when I was filled with uncertainty about how I was going to pay my rent, afford paper, or pay other bills. John Rutter, President of Country Dinner Playhouse, contracted my professional services and even took me to lunch once a month to console me and support my endeavor. Sometimes when I was feeling down and doubtful, the luncheon appointment was the highlight of my week. He has always been a loyal and respectful friend.

In a single two-hour session, my gifted friend Russell McGregor provided unusual clarity to the birthing of the Three-Step Process for Integrating Courage. Roberta Nayfack is a loyal friend and dedicated supporter from my years when I lived in West Los Angeles. She called every week to make sure I was hanging in there. "Aunt Gert" Pepper read my manuscripts even with the loss of vision in one eye. In her eighties, she cheered me up with her steadfast positive attitude.

I am forever indebted to these specific friends and all the other friends and acquaintances, including Judith Cahan, Judy Watson, Cindy Musil, Susan VanDorsten, Jalynn Venis, Eva Shaw, Jan DeSanti, and Kris Wenzel, who kept saying, "You go, girl."

A special acknowledgment goes to Margaret Maupin, Front List Buyer, for the Tattered Cover Book Store for bestowing the first words of encouragement and a written testimonial.

My 486 laptop died as I was on the last leg of finishing the book, but once again a set of reaching hands appeared. Russ gave me a new laptop, and the uncertainty about finishing the book began to fade.

Keslie Lamkin's gifted spirit arrived toward the end of my yellow brick road. She completed the last changes of the book perfectly and professionally.

Bona Dea (Italian for Good Goddess) Publishing was launched to distribute *Courage* for a year. It was embraced by the wonderful Tattered Cover Book Store, and made the bestseller list there for many months. It was one of the winners of the Colorado Independent Publishers Association award.

A truly golden brick in the long and winding road was Executive Editor Lauren Marino of Broadway Books, to whom I had the courage to send an unsolicited review copy of my book. The rest is history. Lauren didn't skip a beat to snatch me up, and graciously referred me to agent Mary Ann Naples. In a few days, I had the best editor in the publishing industry and an agent. Both understood how I use my own courage to manifest my visions. I thank both of them for perceiving value in my life's purpose and for their team contribution, along with Cate Tynan, Betsy Areddy, Heather Flaherty, and Catherine Pollock.

I would have risked losing my courage without the love and support of my family members, my mother Corine, my sister Debbee, my brother Michael, and the spirits of my father Tommy and brother Steven. Aunt Marilyn read every edition and devotedly thought they were all great. Everyone who touched my life during these years, whether clients or friends, provided the green lights that urged me to keep going.

May you always be blessed. I love you all.

INTRODUCTION

Tears are evidence of lost courage.

Sandra Ford Walston

EVERY WOMAN'S JOURNEY OF DISCOVERY

This book is about women and courage—how women can begin to live their lives more fully by discovering and reclaiming the virtue of courage. It specifically helps women to develop courage as a resource, to learn how to draw often on that resource, and to teach others to do so.

Incorporating real stories of contemporary women who have called on courage to transform their lives, this book is more than a catalyst for change. It provides an inspirational blueprint to help women achieve growth through understanding and embracing courageous attitudes and actions.

The women quoted in this book are not famous; they are every woman. You will see how, having become aware of their own courage, they followed their convictions, took risks, faced the future, and pursued their dreams. As you, too, discover your courage, you will build the tools necessary to create the life you desire.

Courage is the finest virtue, the heart and spirit of life.

Courage is the finest virtue, the heart and spirit of life. The purpose of this book is to *en*courage every woman to identify and access her own reservoir of

1

courage, reclaim the power of the heart, and integrate both into her feminine energy.

My life experiences are similar to those of other women who encounter the normal bumps and bruises of living. Yet I feel that an invisible ally that may elude many women has guided me. From an early age, I recognized and cherished the energy of courage. When faced with crises in my life, I discovered that I could always count on courage to help me with the constant reinvention of my being. I have drawn on courage to overcome illness, reveal vulnerability, face obstacles, and confront abuse.

I first became aware of my own courage when I was five years old. A rare form of chicken pox threatened my life. My parents rushed me to a hospital where I lapsed into unconsciousness for a week. I was so ill that the doctors told my parents I might not live. The experience left me not only with physical scars but a profound awareness that if I could overcome critical illness, I could overcome almost anything. This budding awareness, which I now know was a burgeoning reservoir of courage, continued to strengthen and sustain me through many phases of my life.

Another pivotal event occurred when I was twenty. As a Catholic, I was taught to abstain from sexual activity before marriage. Nevertheless, I became pregnant out of wedlock. The pregnancy was a lonely and terrifying ordeal. For three months, I persevered through morning sickness that lasted all day long, and dry heaves forced me to throw up in street gutters as I walked to college classes. Honoring my faith, I felt compelled to go to confession and absolve myself of what I considered a sin. Movies depicting women dying during childbirth had made an impression on my young mind, and I feared that I might die before being absolved of my wrongdoing. Desperately distraught and confused, I didn't know which way to turn. But after much introspection, I was able to confront my disgrace and face a priest.

Entering the confessional with tears of shame, I told the priest of my dilemma. Remarkably, he told me, "God has forgiven you, but you have not forgiven yourself." In that moment, I was filled with an enormous sense of relief and comfort. I realized I had the power of choice. I did not want to marry someone I did not love, nor did I want an abortion. So, with great pain and internal struggle, I decided to give my baby up for adoption. Nothing has compared to going home from the hospital with empty arms.

My experience with the priest turned out to be a monumental blessing. From that experience, my "courageous will" became real to me, and my consciousness of the power of courage provided me with a tool I have used all my life.

Years later, as an adult, I followed a man I was to marry from California to Colorado, where he established a new business. While a major move can be a difficult transition for anyone, this adjustment was greatly complicated by a painful breakup shortly after our relocation.

Angry, disillusioned, and completely *dis*couraged, I had to face the unknown. I was profoundly frightened by the instability of my life, and there I was in a city where I had no friends, family, or job. My core fear was that I would not survive. If I did survive, how could I persevere under the circumstances?

I felt vulnerable, fragile and abandoned. Many times, while flying to visit my family for the holidays, I prayed the plane would crash. If I died, my disheartened spirit would no longer be in pain. I would not be required to reinvent myself.

Yet, in moments of prayer and meditation, I kept hearing an internal voice offering hope: If you can make it through this depressing ordeal, great insight and a special gift will unfold.

This crisis reawakened my awareness of courage as a force that I needed to survive. With courage, a devastating experience could be redeemed as a source of fresh insight, clarity, and purpose. This turning point convinced me that God had put me on this planet to sharpen and evolve the courageous spirit within me, and to encourage other women to do the same.

HEART'S PASSION

As I matured, I was keenly interested in developing self-awareness. Observing how I approached the normal transitions of my life, I noted that my ally— courage—served me well. I made drastic career changes every six to eight years, and each industry I entered was significantly different from the last. Yet as I moved through the fields of education, real estate, banking, and business consulting, I was able to transfer my skills with relative ease from one business sector to another.

When asked how I could so easily maneuver through these career transitions, I replied that the desired outcomes were easy for me to envision and implement as long as I drew upon my heart's desire and my courage. In each industry I was motivated by the excitement of working on my own. Creativity, an essential element of my character, partnered with my courage to "invent" both my professional and personal life.

Assisting others is a goal in my life, whether as a friend, consultant, speaker, coach, or author. Fascination with the richness of life and a deep commitment to upholding the highest of human values have been the threads from which I have woven my life experience. I experience all aspects of my life with passion. I challenge myself beyond the status quo, pushing for excellence in sports, travel, relationships, writing, and speaking.

For a long time, I didn't realize that this approach to life was unusual. Living life with gusto seemed natural, innate. But I know, now, that is not so. Living life with verve is a cultivated skill. With courage as my strength, I have been able to design meaningful goals for my life. And doing so has enabled me to claim my heart and spirit.

Writing has never been one of my ambitions. I am a public speaker and prefer to express myself orally, so writing this book has been one of my two greatest acts of courage. The other was giving up my son for adoption. Thanks to that wonderful and caring priest who helped me, I mustered the courage I needed to forge ahead. I knew even then that nothing would ever be as difficult as that devastating experience.

As a five-year-old, a young adult, and a grown woman, I used my courage to reinvent myself. As I continued to nurture the courage I discovered during those particularly difficult times, courage became an invaluable companion during the more ordinary trials of life.

During the many times I edited this section of the book, I become aware that I was crying. I was crying about the first half of my life, and I realized the tears were evidence of lost courage—the times I did *not* draw from my reservoir of courage.

With a vulnerable heart filled with courage, I dedicate this book to my son, always loved and never forgotten; his memory gives me the courage to do what I am called to do.

WHY WOMEN AND COURAGE?

I wrote this book to help women understand what courage really is, why society rarely recognizes women as courageous, and why such recognition is vital to knowing ourselves. Discovering courage awakens an ancient feminine energy that every woman should utilize. Reading this book and working through the three-step process (see Chapter Six) can be a major step in integrating courage into your life.

Discovering courage awakens an ancient feminine energy that every woman should utilize.

Courage: The Heart and Spirit of Every Woman challenges women to expand their self-perceptions and adopt courage as one aspect of a complete self. When a woman recognizes her conditioned responses—when she ceases to be a product of the past and calls upon the aid and comfort of courage—she will tap a reservoir of energy. Then, and only then, can courage serve as the catalyst for transforming obstacles into opportunities.

In this book you will read stories of real women who share their intimate experiences in manifesting courage. The women interviewed come from diverse backgrounds, and there is no correlation between courage and age, ethnic background, or education (see Research and Survey Results on page 56).

The years of interviews yielded the Source Wheel (see page 86), which depicts twelve Behaviors of Courage. Specific action techniques can be used to integrate courage and enjoy the benefits of doing so. A special section called Books Recomended by the Courageous Women has been prepared as an additional resource for your journey.

By fusing courage with their innate energy, all women can enhance their ability to act from their hearts. When confronted with a choice, you can consciously call on courage as a guiding force. And by understanding how other women have used this forgotten virtue, you can gather energy to meet challenging experiences, expand your perceptions, and enrich your life.

By fusing courage with their innate energy, all women can enhance their ability to act from their hearts.

EVERY WOMAN

All women have had debilitating experiences that compel self-examination and reinvention. Many emotional, physical, and psychological crises are common to women cross-culturally: fear, loss, illness, abuse, betrayal, and low self-esteem. Yet the courage to face and conquer these obstacles is available to every woman.

Courage: The Heart and Spirit of Every Woman is a powerful tool for discovering a new force, acknowledging an existing one, or recovering a lost one. Allow its images to open your mind to a more spirited and joyful way of living. Then take what you need from its passages to fill your heart and spirit. It is for every woman. And every woman is you.

COURAGE

teaches women
how to tap
into their own
reservoirs of courage
to live their lives
more fully.

Courage

Opens

Untapped

Reservoirs

And

Generates

Energy.™

PART ONE

REFLECTION

REFLECTION

"I want to go home," Dorothy wailed as she clutched Toto. "You'll never go home, my pretty," cackled the Wicked Witch of the West. "You must pay for what you did."

"But I didn't mean to do it," Dorothy said as the dark figure flew away on her broom and she was left alone. "What are we going to do, Toto? We'll never get to Kansas. Never. Never. Never."

So begins a classic tale—of courage.

The Wonderful Wizard of Oz, one of the most beloved books of the twentieth century, was made into a movie more than sixty years ago, yet this classic story of a young girl's courageous journey still applies, metaphorically, to women today. Dorothy's journey symbolizes a basic human quest in each of us—to find the courage that will help us through life.

As we strive to find our own place "over the rainbow," we encounter many hurdles and helpers along the way. In Oz, Dorothy and her dog, Toto, encounter Glinda the Good Witch, the Scarecrow, the Tin Man, and the Cowardly Lion. They join forces to gain strength and support and to search for the source that will make them whole.

In the storybook journey, each one makes

choices about which direction to take and how to handle distractions along the Yellow Brick Road. At each turn, they ask the question, "Now which way do we go?" Dorothy, resolutely seeking the truth, discovers through their collaborative effort that all she ever needed to find her way home was her own courage.

"You've always had the power, my dear. You've always had the power."

In real life, each of us must discover the answers to our own questions. As the Good Witch reminded Dorothy, "You've always had the power, my dear. You've always had the power."

CHAPTER ONE

OVERCOMING THE MYTH

*Man enjoys the great advantage of having a god
endorse the code he writes; and since man exercises
a sovereign authority over women it is especially
fortunate that this authority has been vested in him
by the Supreme Being . . . the fear of God will
therefore repress any impulse towards
revolt in the downtrodden female.*

Simone de Beauvoir
The Second Sex, 1949

THE COURAGEOUS GODDESS

The stories that are told about women influence our
understanding about ourselves and provide us either with boundaries or inspiration for achieving
great feats. Early history was passed on through the
oral tradition. The stories about men and women
were told around the fires at night or were imparted
to the young during rites of initiation. However, as
*hist*ory began to be written, men were the ones who
wrote down the important events of the community
because women were not taught how to read or
write. These scribes preserved history from their
perspective and determined which events should be
remembered. Those scribes—both ancient and
modern—have placed the events of history in a
context that has shaped the destiny of generations
of women. As we understand the changing context

of history, we can begin to rewrite our own stories and emphasize the history of women who are courageous in extraordinary and ordinary times.

In the days when history was recounted around the family fires, people worshiped a supreme female creator. Beginning with the Neolithic period around 7000 B.C., women, revered as wise, valiant, powerful, just, and immortal, were honored. They were called by many names, including the Great Goddess, Divine Ancestress, Mother Goddess, Creatress of Life, Mistress of Heaven, Our Lady, and High Priestess. The female's ability to produce a child made her the object of the male's worship; women were the magical birth-givers and breast-feeders who nurtured the young.

About the time agricultural communities began to develop (women were the food gatherers and generally accepted as being responsible for the development of agriculture), the males' role in conception was recognized as a biological one. Childbirth was no longer seen as magical. This awareness decreased female worship.

As men moved forward, women stepped back into the shadows. Men, bolstered by their superior strength and their misunderstanding of biology, grew to believe that it was the man—the father—who was solely responsible for conceiving a child. The mother was now a mere vessel who accepted the man's seed and carried the child to term.

Simplistically speaking, the notion that men were solely responsible for conception formed the core belief that justified patriarchy. Women were considered the husband's "property." Over time, the idea that men were destined to be in charge was accepted as the way things are and always have been.

Not until the scientific advances of the nineteenth century, when biologists demonstrated that both male and female shared equally in conceiving a child, was the concept of parity between men and women seriously considered. Women began, in baby steps, the move toward equality.

But women have always held places of honor in ancient history (or *herstory*, as you might call it). Ancient legends describe the Goddess as a powerful, courageous leader in battle, and an intelligent, wise counselor. The classical Greeks worshiped Athena, a bold and beautiful warrior, and the huntress Artemis lived in fierce purity without men. The Greeks also believed in the existence of Amazons, a band of savage females who fought valiantly on the battlefield. And because goddesses were honored for their skills at battle and in counsel, women of those times yearned to be like them.

Merlin Stone states in her book *When God Was a Woman* that the female divinity was "revered as warrior or hunter, courageous soldier, or agile markswoman who was sometimes described as possessing the most 'curiously masculine' attributes, the implication being that her strength and valor made her something of a freak or physiological abnormality" as compared to male warriors. Some myths state that the Amazons had a physiological abnormality—they cut off one breast to be better archers.

But women have always held places of honor in ancient history (or herstory, *as you might call it).*

THE REVERED WOMAN

What was life like for women in a society that worshiped a brave and wise female deity? They emulated her. Women held positions of respect and status. Intuitive and in touch with both their intellect

and their emotions, they counseled others at
shrines. Women owned businesses. Laws allowed
possessions and real estate to be passed to daughters. Some laws allowed women to have two husbands and other laws permitted a man to be
executed if he raped a woman.

However, as communities embraced monothe-
ism, matriarchies declined. Women's rights and their
shrines became less sacred. The Great Goddess became the subservient consort of the invaders' male
gods, who usurped her power. Patriarchy—along
with worshipping a supreme male deity—gradually
suppressed and destroyed the ancient Goddess religions and women's status. As a result, laws con-
cerning women changed and a woman's right to
engage in economic activities diminished. New laws
dictated what women could inherit and what could
be passed on to children. These laws also strictly
governed abortion, rape, virginity, and infidelity.
Eventually, women were completely devalued.

Over the centuries, it became the norm for property to pass only through the father's line of succes-
sion. Patriarchal systems of religion and law led to
misogyny, the hatred of women and all that women
represented. Indeed, as Merlin Stone so cleverly observes, "We may find ourselves wondering to what
degree the suppression of women's rites has actually been the suppression of women's rights."

OH, WHERE DID ALL THE GODDESSES GO?

What caused the disappearance of goddesses from
the ancient Western world? In a word, patriarchy.
But the loss of the concept of goddess symbolized
greater losses.

In *The Alphabet Versus the Goddess: The Conflict*

Between Word and Image, Leonard Shlain, M.D., states, "I was struck by the thought that the demise of the Goddess, the plunge in women's status, and the advent of harsh patriarchy and misogyny occurred around the time that people were learning how to read and write."

While the death of the Goddess diminished the status of all mortal women, "more critical was the destruction of those symbolic, political, familial, and religious sources of power traditionally associated with women," writes Mary Condren in *The Serpent and the Goddess*. "This would be the precondition for the new society to take root, a society where women would take it upon themselves to give birth; where women would be firmly under control; and where kings, warriors, and priests would develop elite forms of power, effectively abolishing or superseding the power structure of the clan systems." The last temple celebrating the Goddess was destroyed around 500 A.D.

LET'S BLAME EVE

Since the fall of women from divine worship, most religions have taught that God is male. In the Western world, the Torah and the Bible feature few stories that favorably depict women. In fact, the Bible begins with the story of Adam betrayed by the temptress Eve. This myth, perpetuated through the ages, blames woman for the "fall of man," and offers it as a convenient excuse for the ills of mankind. Even today, people keep women in subservient roles via a subtle belief system that female sin led—and leads—men astray. Such a position is further justified by the Bible, which quotes the obvious punishment—the pain of childbirth. Genesis

Since the fall of women from divine worship, most religions have taught that God is male.

17

3:16 reads, "in pain you shall bring forth children, yet your desire shall be for your husband and he shall rule over you."

This myth, Stone reminds us, was propagated to provide divine sanction for male superiority. She offered personal examples from her own childhood to show how parents and religious authorities misuse scripture. "Instead of receiving compassion and sympathy or admiring respect of courage," Stone writes, "I was to experience this pain as guilt, the sin of my wrongdoing laid heavily upon me as punishment for simply being a woman, a daughter of Eve."

The male's divine right to dominate his wife also has survived for centuries. According to Stone, "Once the economic security of women became undermined by male-dominated power in society, women were forced to accept one stable male provider as the one who ruled the roost."

Many myths continue to hold enormous power by focusing on earlier restrictions. Riane Eisler writes in *Sacred Pleasure*, "We will certainly be amazed that our most famous story of human origins, the Genesis story of Adam and Eve, has absolutely nothing good to say about sex, love, or pleasure, that it presents the human quest for higher consciousness as a curse rather than a blessing, and that it does not even touch on the awe and wonder we humans experience when we behold or touch someone we love."

TODAY'S HEROINES WEAR LEATHER BRASSIERES

Myths offer ideas that guide us when we are young and easily influenced. In 1998, *Xena: Warrior Princess* was television's highest-rated first-run drama. Xena appealed to millions of viewers as a "don't-mess-with-me," brains-and-beauty warrior dressed in leather. She is good, and she is strong, albeit shadowed by a questionable past in which she made mistakes she cannot change. Lucy Lawless, the New Zealand actress who starred as Xena, noted that this courageous warrior princess is portrayed as "a woman with the devil on her shoulder, constantly fighting the darker side of her own nature." With her sidekick Gabrielle representing the tender side of a warrior, they "kick butt" as role models for young girls today.

Ironically, this strong woman concept reflects the limits of progress for women in the twenty-first century. Rather than seeing strength and courage as part of the gentle fabric and soul of any woman, such images depict courage as unusual and atypical, and usually with a masculine bravado. Though Xena exemplifies the tenet that, despite the past, women can find their courage and fight for their dreams, the "kick butt" attitude fails to teach young women how to build strength of character and inner resources to overcome adversity in everyday life and to do it in a way that is more complimentary to their feminine natures. Indeed, we will know that we have achieved equality when women are noted and praised for their unique brand of steadfast courage. Only then will we, as a society, mend the frayed fabric of modern life.

CULTURAL SANDS DO SHIFT

Women who exhibit the traditional characteristics, i.e., masculine characteristics of courage, are seen as aggressive, overbearing, and unladylike—traits heavily *dis*couraged. Even today, certain cultural and religious beliefs forbid women from displaying

Indeed, we will know that we have achieved equality when women are noted and praised for their unique brand of steadfast courage.

this type of courage. In some societies, women must worry about their very presence causing discord among peers, family members, or religious leaders. The prohibitions against speaking up are so strong that some feel uncomfortable when speaking out woman-to-woman against injustice.

Given the common understanding that men are more inclined to be courageous and women are more likely to be docile, many women remain reluctant to expose their own potent individual courage. The courageous acts of women like Joan of Arc, who was burned at the stake in the fifteenth century for her beliefs and her zeal, seem extraordinary. Every culture subtly teaches women to make choices consistent with the norms of the day, and most contemporary cultures extol silence and passivity as feminine virtues. As for Joan of Arc, the lesson her story teaches, if we do not dive below the surface, is that strong women get burned.

Every culture subtly teaches women to make choices consistent with the norms of the day, and most contemporary cultures extol silence and passivity as feminine virtues.

Challenging the long-held myths of the past is the first step to shifting cultural norms. To courageously question such myths is to crack the silence that has kept women in denial of their finest strengths. Women everywhere are rising up as they see these myths for what they are. In time, society will recognize women's collective courageous acts and banish the unwritten rules that keep women from realizing their personal courage. But changes in myths and realities go hand in hand with behavioral changes in our lives. That is why it is so important to refashion our own scripts and the images that clutter our minds. By doing that, we can courageously reclaim the female creative power.

The challenges of today do not require a metal

shield like the one used by Xena, Warrior Princess. Like Dorothy in *The Wonderful Wizard of Oz,* we have always had our own courage. Nurtured within, that personal strength becomes an invisible shield for the heart and spirit of every woman.

CHAPTER TWO

THE FORGOTTEN VIRTUE

*Life shrinks or expands in proportion
to one's courage.*

Anaïs Nin

COURAGE BOUND BY NARROW DEFINITION

In contemporary usage, the word *courage*—from the Old French *corage* (heart and spirit)—means bravery. This definition narrows courage to one facet: facing and dealing with danger. But in earlier times, courage meant mental or moral strength to venture, to persevere, and to withstand danger, fear, or difficulty. If this broader definition of courage prevailed, women would be viewed much differently today. This is the definition you are reclaiming!

A TRAIT ASSOCIATED WITH MALES

The impoverished view of courage that pervades society today would have us believe that courage is solely a male trait. Pulp fiction, comic books, action-oriented television shows, and films have all contributed to this male-dominated view. Blockbuster action movies tell us that courage is found predominantly in "real" men on the screen—spies, cops, detectives, gunfighters, and soldiers. This Superman type of courage faces adversity with superb strength, bulging muscles, assertive behavior, and physical skill. Courageous male roles such as Agent

But in earlier times, courage meant mental or moral strength to venture, to persevere, and to withstand danger, fear, or difficulty.

007 from the James Bond movies are portrayed as rock-solid characters—also, great lovers with huge sexual appetites—as well as constant risk-takers who react swiftly to conquer the bad guy. Watching the moves of superheroes in violent action pictures, a young boy logically aspires to be a "he-man" when he grows up, an ambition further encouraged by action figures such as GI Joe Extreme, which sport massive arms with rippling muscles.

These images intensify the myth that says men have to prove themselves in the arenas of war, work, and women. Popular male icons perpetuate the beliefs that men are independent while women are dependent, that men dominate while women yield, that men make history while women provide them with an audience for emotional support.

Conversely, females are depicted in movies, television, magazines, and commercials as fashion-oriented, pretty, vulnerable, tender, thin but big-busted, and sexy above all else.

Emerging over time, modern media has intensified these false distinctions between men and women. Portraits of Victorian women featured their beauty and the ideals of womanliness. The women were somebody's wife, daughter, or sister, and were called "fancy subjects." The portraits of men revealed their accomplished character: forcefulness, ruggedness, and manliness. Men qualified as objects for portraiture by their prominence and attainment; women by their attractiveness. Imagine a book of women's portraits in which none could be identified as beautiful or none as having feminine traits as conveyed through beauty. Then label their expressions as some aspect of courage: determination, forthrightness of verbal expression, unrelenting

Emerging over time, modern media has intensified these false distinctions between men and women.

23

convictions, or downright gutsy. No longer would women be immortalized by just beauty. Character would play a key role to change what women can do and can do well.

Merlin Stone comments, "Man gained the image of the one who accomplishes the greatest and most important deeds, while woman was relegated the role of ever-patient helper and subsequently assured that this was the natural state of female-male relationships." The new economic realities that oblige most women to work outside their homes, even though most occupations are still gender-labeled, have done the most to change the stereotypes.

STEREOTYPICAL COURAGE

Courage is much more complex than spontaneous reactions to traumatic events.

Courage is much more complex than spontaneous reactions to traumatic events. Certainly courage is involved when a person dives into a lake to save a drowning person or acts as a human shield in the line of fire, risking or incurring death to save the lives of others. However, as long as our image of courage is limited to such stereotypes, society's perceptions will resist change, and all of us will be deterred from recognizing our potential as courageous people able to transcend ongoing difficulties in our lives.

Small acts often require great courage. When Sheryl, age thirty-seven, told her boss that she was going to be interviewed for a book on courageous women, he asked how many people she had saved from being mugged. He then let her know he had saved three people from assault. For Sheryl, being interviewed demonstrated courage. She felt vulnerable and awkward. She shared that her most recent challenge was losing weight. She had lost weight before and gained it back. Through courage she claimed victory.

"I realized that getting control of my weight allowed me control of the rest of my life. My courage gives me strength to persevere," Sheryl said.

Sometimes just being a woman takes courage. Debra, a thirty-three-year-old single mother with a master's degree, said, "Women make ethically right choices based on their beliefs and understandings. In the working world, women hold themselves to a high benchmark. If they don't think they can reach it, they don't see themselves as courageous. I now wonder what difference it would have made in my decisions if I had thought of myself as courageous a long time ago."

As you learn how to access your *cor*, your strong heart, while handling challenges encountered on the path of life, you foster belief in your own inner resources. Small courageous acts accumulate like drops of rain in a puddle to create your own vast reservoir of courage.

Small courageous acts accumulate like drops of rain in a puddle to create your own vast reservoir of courage.

APPLYING A BROADER DEFINITION

"Why is a woman's courage defined differently from a man's courage?" asked Myrna, a thirty-year-old married woman with a daughter.

"I don't think it's right that people make courage a gender-oriented word. When discussing courage, most people want to clarify whether you're talking about a male or female before they will say whether they are or aren't courageous. I think we all have courage within us. My courage is there when I choose to draw on it. I believe society makes a woman choose not to be courageous because it's mostly used as a male adjective or label."

Linda, a poised, articulate forty-six-year-old, offered this view of courage. "Women's courage comes from inner strength and inner guidance and being able to handle what challenges them on a daily basis. The small things that challenge us, nonetheless, take what I call courage as opposed to acts of valor. In my opinion, men think about courage as valor, such as in sporting events or war. With maturity, my spiritual outlook has expanded to include the lyrics 'a woman has the strength of ten thousand men.' There have certainly been times I wished the man I was with would face daily challenges with courage!"

Jody, forty-seven, is married with three children and works for the Department of Social Services. She said that one of the biggest revelations she experienced was learning that courage was at the core of everything. "It takes courage for me to be honest with my feelings. It takes courage to be fair to the employees I manage," she said.

"Sometimes it takes courage for me to be outgoing. Many times I take a stand to use my intuition to make decisions. Sometimes I don't like what I find out, but at least I know the truth."

THINKING HIGH, WIDE, AND UNIQUELY

Embracing the broader definition of courage makes sense for society, in general, and women, in particular. The mental or moral strength to venture, persevere, conquer fear, and withstand difficulty can transform each life's journey. Roberta's comment reflects this broader view: "All women are courageous, even though they may not think they are.

Any woman who raises children, who lives her own life, and who is the sole provider—that, to me, is courageous!"

Philosopher Alasdair MacIntyre, in *After Virtue*, defines courage as a virtue, drawing a direct connection between courage and concern for other individuals, communities, and causes. As women redefine courage, they learn to recognize and nourish it in themselves. When women consciously possess courage, they take heart in whatever circumstance life sends them, and begin to express themselves in exciting, new ways. They speak up when they feel overlooked, they make tough choices that suit their desires, and they face their vulnerability with strength and perseverance.

As women redefine courage, they learn to recognize and nourish it in themselves.

Courage, Michael Robbins believes, leads to a vital and abundant sense of living. As he says in his book *Tapestry of the Gods*, "When one takes heart, one realizes that the imperishable life force sustains all and can never be exhausted; thus courage is born. It is the flow of life, the energy manifested as cosmic electricity or 'Fire Electric,' which is the ultimate source of all strength and courage."

WHY COURAGE IS THE FORGOTTEN VIRTUE

Women possess courage in abundance, but often they do not perceive this virtue as courage nor call it courage—just as the Cowardly Lion in *The Wizard of Oz* did not acknowledge his natural courage. Why is it that the lion's share of women do not see themselves as courageous? It seems the power and beauty of womanly courage have been long forgotten.

Courage is the forgotten virtue because women do not recognize their everyday actions as significant.

Courage is the forgotten virtue because women do not recognize their everyday actions as significant. If every woman identified the acts she performs every day as courageous, she would be able to use that same courage to transform her life and accomplish her heart's desire. When every woman takes the time to define what courage means in the lives of others she knows, she will discover that this virtue is also available to her.

ROLE MODELS FOR COURAGE

Fortunately, movies like *The Wizard of Oz* provide role models for both girls and boys. Carol, married, forty-nine, a former English instructor now succeeding in her own business, truly loves this movie. When she saw it as a young girl, she identified immediately with the Cowardly Lion. It seemed strange to her that a lion would seek courage—a quality a lion was presumed to own. That irony was reflected in her own life.

"Like the Cowardly Lion, my behavior and outer shell reflected a false pretense of being courageous, but inside I was very intimidated and scared of the world around me. Watching the movie provided me with support. I was thrilled that the Lion did indeed find the courage he was lacking. Therefore, I could too."

In 1998, when the movie was re-released in digitally remastered form, Carol again felt an affinity for the Lion. He shudders and moans in his Brooklyn accent, "I haven't any courage. I am even afraid of myself. If I only had the noive!" But the Lion is forced to face all his fears as he travels through the dark forest, and as he and his determined companions get closer to the Emerald City, he gains confidence that he will find his answer and reclaim his courage. Finally, the Cowardly Lion is awarded a medal for his courage, and he bursts out, "Read what my medal says—'Courage, ain't it de truth.'"

Carol was fortunate in realizing her kinship with the Cowardly Lion. She felt like a victim who had been kept from claiming her courage by feelings of fear. But, she continues: "When the Lion knew he had to rescue Dorothy from the Wicked Witch, he realized he had to follow through with the heroic task by tapping his source of inner knowledge that he was 'the King.' This displayed his ability to be courageous in the face of distress."

Carol now practices courage daily to empower her in all of her decisions. For her, courage is an ingrained belief or faith. While making the choice to develop her own sense of courage was not easy, she is now certain that her courage can never be taken away from her. Like the Lion, Carol has recognized her fear and asked for help.

"When I do what it takes to face obstacles, believing everything will work out, as it did for the Lion, courage becomes the virtue that pulls me through tough situations. I believe that it is not found in the opinion of another, like the Wizard, but in the core character inside of me. This is true for us all."

"When I do what it takes to face obstacles, believing everything will work out, as it did for the Lion, courage becomes the virtue that pulls me through tough situations."

THE PRICE YOU PAY FOR OUTDATED DEFINITIONS

Holding on to a definition of courage that restricts acts of valor to dangerous situations limits our outreach, while adopting the broader definition honors us in our everyday acts of courage. The women quoted above were eager to mention just a few of the acts they considered courageous: raising children, living alone, facing fear, being honest with feelings, being fair to others, and listening to intuition.

The courage that is every woman's birthright has been forgotten in a world where women's virtues are devalued. Yet, with women changing roles and stereotypes, a new feminine energy cannot be far behind. Women are at a turning point at the beginning of this new millennium. In an article "The Future Is Ours to Lose," Naomi Wolf writes: "Women have been trained to see themselves as having no relationship to history, and no claim upon it. Feminism can be defined as women's ability to think about their subjugated role in history, and then to do something about it. The twenty-first century will see the End of Inequality—but only if women absorb the habit of historical self-awareness, becoming a mass of people who, rather than do it all, decide at last to change it all. The future is ours to lose. We are at a critical turning point."

Historians call these turning points in history "open moments." Acknowledging ourselves as courageous marks the spot. How much do you have to lose if you do not take steps immediately to acknowledge yourself as courageous?

"Women have been trained to see themselves as having no relationship to history, and no claim upon it."

CHAPTER THREE

INNATE OR ACQUIRED?

Whatever God has brought about
is to be borne with courage.

Sophocles

WHERE DOES COURAGE COME FROM?

During many years of investigating courage, I found
that, more than any other human virtue, courage
walks hand in hand with vulnerability, responsibility to one's self, truthfulness, respect, faith, and love.
I wondered how women activated their courage,
and I was curious to learn if this beneficial virtue
was innate or acquired. Why do some have it while
others do not?

IS COURAGE INNATE IN WOMEN . . . ?

For Tracy, one of the women interviewed for this
book, a combination of courage and self-esteem is
the foundation of her core self. During the interview, she displayed grace, dignity, and an uncanny
self-assurance. Her stellar educational background
supported her demeanor. A graduate of Boston
College and Georgetown Law School, this forty-
three-year-old African-American woman exuded
charisma. Her point of view leaves no doubt that
she is an achiever.

"Self-esteem is the most important aspect of courage."

"My innate courage and my self-esteem work together. Self-esteem is the most important aspect of

31

courage. I am fearless and have great self-esteem. Being fearless overrides any negative attitudes—I never have the feeling that I can't do something because someone has said it's going to be difficult or painful. I always believe that I can do anything I want to do."

There was never a point in Tracy's life when she perceived herself as fearful. Her parents provided a loving home environment, but her father cautioned her against being too opinionated. She said, "It never occurred to me to withhold my opinions of what is right and wrong. I didn't wake up suddenly and say to myself, 'Stand up and be courageous despite the consequences because it's the right thing to do.' My courage was innate."

Still, an early role model for Tracy was her good-natured grandmother. Strong-willed and hard working, her grandmother did whatever it took to meet the obstacles of life head on. This take-charge approach provided a value system that backed up Tracy's natural assertiveness. "You miss a lot of opportunities by holding back from living life to the fullest," Tracy says. "That's not going to be me!"

Women who allow themselves to embody courage are able to reevaluate their lives . . .

Women who allow themselves to embody courage are able to reevaluate their lives and embark upon a healthy separation from those who no longer support their development. Often, these women must dare to differ from the traditional female role models.

Anne, who grew up the seventh in a family of twelve children, also believes courage is innate. When interviewed, she was twenty-nine, a working mother with two children, and divorced. "Courage," she said, "is the ability to wake up every morning and face whatever life brings you.

"Even though I was a tomboy, it took courage to play with my older brothers. My mother nurtured my innate courage. It was based on her values. 'If you believe you can do anything, you can. So long as you give it your best, give it your all, you can do it.' I am passing this attitude to my two children.

"Courage is that internal challenge that makes you struggle and resolve to seek and do new things. The reservoir is inside, waiting to be filled up. I am astounded that women of this generation still believe we are the weaker sex. We are all born with courage. It shows up in infancy when you learn how to roll over. It takes courage to sit up, walk, and talk. Or, as an adult, to accept and overcome a bad day. People are just blind to the virtue. Identifying courage is critical to claiming it!"

> *"People are just blind to the virtue. Identifying courage is critical to claiming it!"*

. . . OR IS COURAGE LEARNED?

Laurie, on the other hand, believes that courage is learned. At age forty-seven, she has no doubt that people are born with certain character traits that predispose them to certain actions. But, she believes, through trial and error, people learn that each action has an effect, good or bad, and thus their responses to a given situation are conditioned.

"I think courage is a learned behavior built on a predisposition. If you watch newborns, you see they have no limits—they're invincible. Babies try new things, they explore, and have no fear. They reach out to touch, taste, and smell, checking their movements with reactions against the environment. I don't think the concept of courage exists for them.

33

If you asked a mother with twins, a boy and a girl, about their different behaviors, I believe she would say the boy was into everything and the girl was hesitant. Some things are part of character and part of nature.

"It is the reward or punishment they receive for their actions that changes the behavior or limits the action. Reaction represents the fundamental split in whether somebody will fail to exhibit courage or will react by accepting more risk to test the limits. Courage is tied to a willingness to risk. There are different levels of risk, from feeling guilty, or upsetting someone else, to losing your ego. I assume that there are two types of courage. Sometimes there is no choice and you have to be courageous, such as in a crisis. The second type of courage may be desiring something or having a dream to pursue. Then you have to overcome inertia, motivating yourself to come out of your comfort zone."

"Courage is tied to a willingness to risk."

IF YOU'VE GOT IT, FLAUNT IT

At least 60 percent of the women I spoke with perceived courage as an innate virtue. For example, Stephie, who heads an organization focused on the advancement of women and the retention of women in senior positions, wholeheartedly believes she was born with courage and that it lives in every woman. Her company highlights the opportunities afforded to women when gender bias is eradicated. According to this dynamic woman, "The issue is to do things in your life that allow courage to flourish and grow to the point where you can hold on to it. I have seen plenty of women who have had courage beaten out of them. But I also have a number of friends whom I consider very courageous.

They have faced challenges by living with an alcoholic parent, struggling academically, or encountering abuse. However, they exude an attitude of: I don't deserve to be treated that way, I won't allow this to happen, and I am going to exert all the influence I can to have this stop."

Myrna, a first-time mother in 1998, also believed she was born with courage. She first displayed her courage when she was six years old. Facing many hardships, she and her grandmother traveled by foot and bus from Guatemala across Mexico to the United States. She recalled her love for her grandmother. "My grandmother was courageous, although I don't think she would be considered so in our society. She raised seven children and was a powerful single woman. This represents a different time and dimension of courage."

"The issue is to do things in your life that allow courage to flourish and grow to the point where you can hold on to it."

After high school in 1990, Myrna, wanting to serve the country she loved, joined the Army against her parents' wishes. Her parents felt that the place for a Hispanic woman was not in the military, but Myrna prevailed. She went to boot camp, then to Germany, and eventually served in Desert Storm in Saudi Arabia.

In boot camp, her drill sergeant encouraged her to be tough. Because she was petite (five feet tall), people doubted her strength and ability. Her height, more than her soft voice and demeanor, forced her to overcome many obstacles. She constantly drew on an inner core of courage. "I showed them my courage by exceeding on my physical training tests," she recalls.

During Desert Storm, Myrna worked in an evacuation hospital as a psychiatric specialist. She helped in other wards by taking care of injured soldiers or prisoners of war and encountered situations that provoked both fear and courage.

"One time our unit arrived first and we were dropped off in an unknown area. The commanders knew it wasn't our designated site. We went into an underground shelter. I could hear Iraqi helicopters hovering above. At that point, I was scared I was going to die, yet I had the courage to face the fear of death. Four agonizing hours later, our unit was picked up and taken to the proper site."

First make yourself aware of courage as a force and a virtue, then practice it, and choose it as a way of life.

As women, we are born with the attributes that allow courage to flourish: strength, fortitude, and motivation. When situations requiring courageous thinking occur with regularity, courage becomes a dominant force in a woman's personality.

Myrna's belief in courage is simple: First make yourself aware of courage as a force and a virtue, then practice it, and choose it as a way of life. Courage becomes an umbrella encompassing all the virtues women possess. That umbrella will also protect the continual growth and self-awareness in every area of life—education, physical and emotional health, motivation, and ambition.

CLAIMING YOUR BIRTHRIGHT

The reservoir of courage and strength resides within each of us. When women give courage permission to surface, they create within themselves a support system. Courage can be perceived as an alternative but friendly path. Women choosing that path feel that life is more under their control and influence. They demand deeper connections and, in essence, redefine their lives.

Myrna believes that setbacks can be turned into

new opportunities. For her, courage is about being optimistic and using your resources to get what you deserve. Courage also means going out on a limb to voice objections under pressure or threatening circumstances.

"When faced with an intimidating situation," Myrna said, "I first learn as much as I can about it, then I can choose or not choose to see it through. The point is, my actions are based on knowledge, not emotions which can lead us astray. A woman once said to me, 'Why are you courageous and I'm not?' I pointed out to her that the mere act of asking a direct question qualifies her as courageous. So, I always advise: Start with small acts of courage, such as asking a challenging question!"

When women give courage permission to surface, they create within themselves a support system.

Karen, a sales manager for an international pharmaceutical company, has used courage as her foundation ever since she can remember. She stated, "Human beings have demonstrated courage over the course of time. The kernel is there. It is in all of us. If it hasn't developed within us, we may have to be taught to recognize courageous acts. Positive support from others reinforces the development of courage. Everyone may not have the ability to reinforce his or her courageous behavior internally."

Karen's mother recognized that standing up for herself in uncomfortable situations was essential. Jewish, and raised in Tennessee, her mother exemplified courage in facing prejudice, and Karen learned to discern and recognize courageous acts. At forty-six years old, Karen shows the same ability to teach courage to her two sons. Her own courage was indispensable when her husband was diagnosed with lung cancer. He had never been a smoker. Bitter and increasingly fearful, he had to have a lung removed and was hospitalized seven times while undergoing chemotherapy.

"All of a sudden he was afraid to do the things he had done before. I pushed him to keep going. I think that is the kind of courage that everyone relates to. Maybe people don't realize that what they are doing demonstrates courage," Karen said.

"Maybe people don't realize that what they are doing demonstrates courage."

The preceding stories highlight a few perspectives on whether courage is innate or learned. But the issue is not as simple as either/or. While courage often seems an innate virtue, we still must learn to cultivate and nurture it. And the fact remains: however you come by it, courage offers a renewable reservoir of hope and strength to draw upon when you need it. Are you ready to create your reservoir or greatly expand what you already have? Will the process be easy? Will it be worth it? Let us look now at how some other women have broken through some old tapes and traps to cultivate and nurture their courage.

CHAPTER FOUR

BLINDING THE EYE
OF THE BEHOLDER

Never grow a wishbone, daughter,
where your backbone ought to be.

Clementine Paddleford

THE TOMBOY MYTH CAN CRAMP YOUR STYLE

Many women grew up with the label "tomboy" attached to their behavior, which meant they were different from the stereotype of ideal womanhood. The negative connotation of being called a tomboy deterred many girls from following their natural inclinations and interests.

For centuries, the men who directed and defined our country also characterized the norm for women. Any traits that differed from the norm placed labels on women identifying them as "other." Most young girls tried to avoid such distinction.

About 20 percent of the women I interviewed described themselves as tomboys—a label demonstrated by strong behavior, particularly in showing athletic ability, preferring boys' games, or having "guts." The etymology of *tomboy* involves two words that generally describe males. Joined into a compound word, *tom* and *boy* originally referred to a "boisterous, rude boy." Before 1553, the word *tom* denoted aggressiveness associated with males, and it was used in the Middle Ages as a term for "common man," based on the often-used name Thomas. In 1579, the term *tomboy* connoted a "bold or immodest woman," and by 1592, a girl who behaved like a spirited, boisterous boy was called a "tomboy."

Furthermore, in *Brewer's Dictionary of Phrase and Fable*, a tomboy is defined as "a romping girl," a term also reserved for a harlot. The term found its way into literature such as Shakespeare's *Cymbeline*, where he writes, "A lady so fair . . . to be partner with tomboys." Today, "tomboy" describes a girl considered boyish or masculine in behavior or manner.

Stephie, growing up in the 1940s and 1950s, labeled herself a bona-fide tomboy. She would not play with dolls or play house like the other girls. Instead, she convinced her friends to play pirates. They all liked to portray the tough-guy roles, such as being captain of the ship.

Looking back, Stephie believes she was born with courage. She saw courageous behavior naturally nurtured in boys but controlled by "should and should not" distinctions for girls. She is convinced her own fortitude gave her a bigger arena in which to play.

"My girl friends didn't do the things I did, nor did they want to play with the boys and do boy stuff. But by playing with the boys, I was pushed physically. I would take risks and break rules. That fit me more naturally. For example, we had a home in the mountains, and I would go horseback riding for six to seven hours. I always took my wire cutters in case I got behind fences and could not get back. Since I was rebellious, I pushed the limits of whatever artificial boundaries were set around me," Stephie said.

Even when playing horses or cowboys, Stephie often took on the role of the stallion, Silver, or the Lone Ranger himself, the famous cowboy of the fifties. She refused to be the innocent maiden who needed to be rescued. She saw herself as the hero and challenged the stereotypes. Stephie sallied forth the arrival of women's ambition. She was not going to be stifled by age-old shackles.

Theresa is forty-five years old and works for one of the leading Fortune 500 companies. She grew up surrounded by restrictive messages.

"I was a tomboy when I was younger, but I learned quickly that it was not a favorable attribute. My fourth grade teacher thought it inappropriate for me to raise my hand to answer questions. It was perceived as bold and too assertive. I just saw myself as vivacious and eager to learn. But in my family, my mother supported comformity. If I expressed an opinion to my parents about my teacher's disapproval, they would punish me for speaking up.

"Any kind of forwardness or strength of character was seen as a bad trait. I was taught not to be courageous!"

"I remember standing in line at the store when I was eight with my mother. I watched her closely observe the cashier ring up our groceries. I asked her if she was intently watching for possible errors by the checkout person. She believed that I was being too daring by asking this innocent question in public. Any kind of forwardness or strength of character was seen as a bad trait. I was taught not to be courageous! But that upbringing never robbed me of my innate courage. Regardless of the labels still attached to my personality, I stand dignified in my courage."

THE POWER OF PERSPECTIVE

Sometimes all it takes to stimulate courage is an accurate view of a situation. Interpreting life is a judgment call based on stored assessments, prejudices, and experiences. As the opinions expressed here show, courage is viewed differently by different people. Shifting your perspective on a long-held belief is difficult. As the years go by, you interpret, verify, and categorize experiences into "assets and liabilities," or "good and bad." The perception of what is good or bad often overpowers the facts in a situation.

Sometimes all it takes to stimulate courage is an accurate view of a situation.

Let me illustrate with a personal example. Once when I was visiting Lauren, a close friend living in Minneapolis, she told me how difficult it was for her to have a discussion with her husband, Rick, without him becoming defensive and creating a conflict. She preferred harmony and nonthreatening exchanges; conflicts made her retreat. So her part of a well-entrenched pattern was to forgo expressing her feelings to avoid a confrontation.

Responding to her frankness, I ventured a suggestion. "Consider Rick's reaction as a personality preference. He is comfortable with anger. Just as some people prefer to please and others prefer to withdraw, he prefers to express anger. Your interpretation of his defensive behavior is your own projected version of an angry response. That's not his reality."

She thought for a moment before replying. "You have always said that all I needed to do was to shift my perspective. But it's sure not easy! Maybe you can help me get started."

We decided to reconstruct a typical conversation that led to a defensive reaction from Rick. I suggested that Lauren recognize Rick's subconscious mode of reacting as simply what it was—confrontational, but for him, comfortable. To get around the problem, Lauren saw that she needed to reframe her perspective. Her preference in conversation was a quiet, give-and-take style. She characterized Rick's preferred style as passionate, emotional, loud, and provocative. Lauren vowed to make allowances for their differences in style and simply listen to hear the true message. Instead of retreating into a cave of resentment, she hoped that, over time, her quiet, yet assertive, lead might inspire Rick to change.

It took great courage for Lauren to consider changing her typical reaction to what she felt were Rick's irrational responses. Her difficulty is a common one. All of us must deal with people every day, people who have different response patterns from our own. We do not feel comfortable dismantling old perceptions to build new ones. We store perceptions from our collective experiences and play them back in our heads like videotapes, over and over again until they become habits. Habits become traps. Lauren was interpreting information based on her way of life.

Habits become traps.

Lauren will not change just because someone suggests that she change. She needs to identify the problem, be inspired to create a different result, and then recognize the benefits of change. The road to self-knowledge is difficult because we all tend to gravitate back to old familiar behavior patterns— even if they make us uncomfortable.

GET RID OF THOSE OLD TAPES AND TRAPS

The process of revelation begins when we initiate

monitoring how the old tapes—the old perceptions—struggle to keep their identity, thus sabotag-
ing new courses of action. A conscious application
of courage can lead to a new approach—when suf-
ficiently motivated. Motivation is the key to changing our perceptions—and our courage. Lauren must
be motivated to improve communication in her
marriage.

When I checked with her later, Lauren told me
our discussion had been an epiphany. The suggestion that she change her perspective made her realize that her approach to her relationship with her
husband had been based on how she "saw" the situation, not the actual "reality." She said, "It never
occurred to me that my reactions were *my* perceptions; I thought they were everyone's reality." She
also realized that others' perceptions are *their* realities—and that not all people share the same reality.

*Courage
comes into
play when we
are digging
for solutions.*

Courage comes into play when we are digging
for solutions. Since Lauren prefers harmony and has
a "need-to-please" demeanor, she needs courage to
create a breakthrough. The breakthrough offers a
reward—a heightened awareness that leads to a different result. Lauren drew on her reservoir of
courage to speak up; she opened a door to her
higher self, and created greater understanding in
her relationship with her husband.

CHAPTER FIVE

ASSESSING THE OLD
"TRIED AND TRUE"

It's not what you do once in a while,
it's what you do day in and day out
that makes a difference.

Jenny Craig

VIRTUES IN TODAY'S COMPLEX WORLD

Homer, the Greek poet, translated the word *arete* as virtue. A fast runner displays the *arete* of his feet in *The Iliad.* While virtue can indeed give wings to your spirit and grant an ease and sureness of task to your life, in modern times it is certainly not limited to athletic prowess. By the twelfth century, virtue in Old French was *vertu* "desirable male qualities, worth, virtue, or virility." In Latin, virtue was *virs,* or energy.

In his autobiography, Benjamin Franklin offered readers a peek at what was to be in his treatise "The Art of Virtue." Even though this article was never published, *The Autobiography of Benjamin Franklin* reveals a system for self-improvement focused on such virtues as silence, sincerity, alertness, calmness, justice, and friendship. Each morning he would ask himself, "What good shall I do today?" He ended each day with the question, "What good have I done today?" and kept a diary in which he recorded his answers. Some scholars feel that

In Latin, virtue was virs, or energy.

Franklin's writing about his thirteen virtues is his greatest literary accomplishment.

Today, virtue has come to mean conformity of one's life and conduct to moral and ethical principles. Mark Twain said, "Always do right. This will gratify some people, and astonish the rest."

Currently, philosopher Alasdair MacIntyre has reintroduced the discussion about virtues. His book *After Virtue* asserts that the core virtues of integrity, justice, and courage should be part of every ethical person's life. He stresses that as a person engages in the practice of life, every action should be examined through the lens of those core virtues. As these virtues are cultivated and interwoven into a person's life, that person becomes an effective, ethical member of the human community.

Professor of business at Regis University in Denver, Colorado, Catharyn Baird, incorporates the discipline of virtue ethics into her business ethics classes and encourages her students to discover these values. "As you determine what is the ethical act and how you want to live," she tells her students, "decide what virtues need to be incorporated into your life and how you can live a life of integrity and courage. As you cultivate the virtues you will become a virtuous person, and decision making will become ever more easy." People who live the examined life find that reviewing their actions against the desired virtues helps convert beliefs into actions.

People who live the examined life find that reviewing their actions against the desired virtues helps convert beliefs into actions.

Regardless of the virtues desired—trust, self-motivation, honesty, humor, compassion, respect, cleanliness, loyalty, determination, or tolerance—most people accept the tenet that a strong human character is a universal good. Looking into your heart, spirit, and mind, and consciously modifying your behavior is essential to becoming a virtuous person. But because virtues are abstract concepts that must be defined and applied to get results, this can be a difficult task.

THE VIRTUE OF PATIENCE

. . . virtues are abstract concepts that must be defined and applied to get results . . .

The question of whether courage is innate or acquired leads to the same question about the origin of other virtues. Take patience, for example. Is patience innate or cultivated? It has been difficult for me to increase my reservoir of patience and integrate this virtue into my life. I always flinch when people think they show support by saying, "Have more patience!"

I once became irritated at a TV commercial in which a company touted its coffee as better than the competitor's because it was roasted slowly. A label above the flaming, rotating roaster read, "Patience is a virtue." I maintain that whether the slow-roasted coffee beans yield a better taste remains a question of personal preference.

With maturity, my patience has increased (slowly, like roasting coffee beans), and I feel I can now recognize more readily when an incident requires me to do nothing. Self-awareness is the key ingredient.

For example, in the early months of writing this book, an agent suggested I refocus the entire project. This meant rethinking and reshaping the whole book. I hit the wall! I became very *dis*couraged. At that point, I gave myself permission to do nothing for four days so I could reclaim my direction, purpose, and courage. My inner voice scolded me, shouting, "You're no good slacking off like this. Get to work!" But it required both patience and courage for me to step back from the project. During this scary period, I had to find the courage to let go of my initial direction. The lack of action made me feel as though I were drifting aimlessly, floating in the most difficult of all courage fields—the unknown. I accepted part of the suggestions made by the agent and used my reliable intuition for the rest.

My insights flow freely when I am vacationing in Bigfork, Montana. My psyche relaxes when I sit on the deck overlooking Flathead Lake. However, I don't often have the luxury of going to my "introvert heaven" in Montana to chill. In this instance, I had to face my doom in my own living room. How could I create an entirely new book proposal and table of contents? I had to call on my inner courage to organize my thoughts and change my perspective. Once my *cor* (heart) got involved, I became *en*couraged again. That change of perspective, merging patience with courage, resulted in this book.

I had to call on my inner courage to organize my thoughts and change my perspective. Once my cor (heart) got involved, I became encouraged again.

THE VIRTUE OF EMPATHY

Empathy is another virtue worth reviewing in the quest for more insight into courage. For many years, I have conducted training on emotional intelligence, called EQ. My presentations include reference to Daniel Goleman's book, *Emotional Intelligence: Why It Can Matter More Than IQ*. One of the factors in one's EQ is empathy. A scientific study featured in Goleman's book suggests that the roots of empathy can be traced to infancy.

But what if empathy was not nurtured in our own childhood? Can we still acquire and use this virtue? The EQ research demonstrates that empathy is connected to self-awareness. The more open we are to our own emotions, the more skillfully we can read other people's feelings. Courage steps onto the same stage.

Linda, who is responsible for career development in a Fortune 500 communications company, helps other women find the courage to face difficult situations. She argues for a connection between empathy and courage: "Having empathy—being able to put ourselves into another's shoes—supports the recognition of one's courage. I provide feedback to employees on how they can improve their promotability, especially when they have failed to advance. This requires sharpened sensitivity, particularly to women managers. Often they stumble in their management style when addressing sensitive subjects, or their need to be liked intermingles with their communication. I encourage them to discuss difficult developmental and behavioral issues with their employees so that they can move ahead. This helps the manager handle difficult situations with grace and empathy."

"Having empathy— being able to put ourselves into another's shoes— supports the recognition of one's courage."

When women managers and their employees take responsibility to act in an ethical manner, the situation changes and trust increases, resulting in heightened personal performance. Courage for Linda has been a behavior learned over time. "I believe courage was demonstrated by the women in my family and became a part of my moral fiber. Through a series of interactions with family members, my character developed."

Linda's mother helped establish the belief system that Linda still follows, and which has blossomed into a set of strong convictions and values. Even today, Linda draws on her mother's advice, "Mom was there saying, 'When it gets tough, keep going.

Setbacks happen.' She also gave me the courage to advance without gender restrictions." Allowed to voice opinions and given the freedom to make mistakes, Linda feels that her family life was unique. She is grateful that the outcome enabled her to have the courage to do what she feels is right. "Courage is one positive facet of life that enhances our culture. Evaluating courage requires monitoring reactions to situations that warrant courage. It is the same as evaluating an individual's level of integrity, or lack of it."

"Courage is one positive facet of life that enhances our culture."

The type of virtue is not what's important. What is important is that your ability to link courage with an empathic sense, sensitivity, and consciousness of what is just and fair, changes how you will think and act.

PART TWO

CREATION

CREATION

OH, EVOLVE!

One day while driving my car, I noticed a bumper sticker that said, "Oh, Evolve!" I immediately wondered how long it had been since I experienced a breakthrough. Had I evolved?

I know that I have evolved. I also know that evolution takes courage. I know that truth from the depths of my heart and spirit.

By studying psychology and esoteric philosophy I realized that my fear of being vulnerable has kept me separated from my spiritual essence. Two theories, the Myers-Briggs Type Indicator® and the Enneagram, helped me gain insight into the patterns of behavior that prevented me from reaching my goals. I was so impressed with the personality preferences, that I became qualified to administer and interpret both theories.

The Myers-Briggs Type Indicator® is an instrument based on the theories of Carl Jung and offers insight into sixteen "personality" preferences based on four scales. The Enneagram theory holds that all people basically fall into one of nine different personality types. The Enneagram describes the different vantage points from which people view the world. These concepts assisted me in discovering my own specific fears.

I learned that if I reveal vulnerability, I will somehow not survive. This fear of not surviving stems from having almost died when I was a child. The fear also seems to compensate for something missing in my life. That missing "something" may be trust. My lack of trust has kept me from being honestly intimate with a partner and myself.

Being aware of my self-perceived limitations was the first step in my transformation. I worked to integrate courage into my life so that I could learn to trust people close to me. I developed a plan and took specific actions to overcome my fear of vulnerability, such as asking for help while writing my book.

Now, as I heal, I have developed a system that others, too, can use. I call it the Three-Step Process for Integrating Courage (see page 59). The process emerged when I decided to pinpoint and interview women who had identified themselves on a survey as being courageous. The survey form was distributed in January 1997 (see page 55). The Research and Survey Results follow this introduction to Part Two.

Further research yielded information about how women

- claim courage,
- identify the faces of courage, and
- generate courage to experience beneficial outcomes.

You can change your perceived limitations. Now that you have explored whether courage is innate or learned, and learned more about stereotypes and the value of other virtues besides courage, let us look at what you see as your perceived traits. Please fill out the survey on the opposite page. Then, you will learn a valuable three-step process for integrating courage. You can discover and reframe whatever uncertainties hold you back and keep you from evolving. You can change your perceived limitations.

SURVEY

Circle nine words that represent your perception of yourself to complete this sentence:

"I PERCEIVE MYSELF TO BE . . ."

charismatic	energetic	conservative	active
honest	goal-oriented	gregarious	reserved
mature	risk-taking	intuitive	approachable
athletic	practical	bold	ordered
humble	fair	happy	determined
intelligent	fulfilled	resilient	visionary
sensible	open-minded	complex	emotional
courageous	moderate	creative	insightful
independent	liberal	private	gutsy

RESEARCH AND SURVEY RESULTS

The purpose of the survey was (1) to support the premise that only 10 to 12 percent of women would perceive themselves as courageous and thereby circle the word, and (2) to identify women who did perceive themselves as courageous, and to tell their stories so others can recognize courage when it appears.

The women identified as courageous were also asked to provide the following information:

1. Give your definition of courage.
2. List personal experiences of courage and any noted behavioral trends behind the actions.
3. Write approximately 120 words on "What courage means to me."

The survey was distributed to a random sampling of women at my training seminars and at women's business meetings. I also gave them to neighbors and friends. All were encouraged to duplicate the survey sheet, pass, mail, or fax it to other women. I wanted to reach the "common" woman, i.e., every woman. I received over seven hundred survey forms. Ages of survey respondents ranged from 21 to 87, with the majority of respondents between the ages of 31 and 50. Ages 21 to 30 were moderately represented, and ages 51 to 60 comprised the smallest group of respondents. Most respondents had attended some college and many had earned degrees.

The research findings supported my prediction that "courageous" is not a common adjective for women to use in describing themselves. Out of almost seven hundred respondents on the survey, only 71 women perceived and described themselves as courageous.

Yet, the survey did suggest that the women who completed the survey had positive perceptions of themselves. The most frequently circled adjectives were:

honest	happy	open-minded	intelligent
determined	intuitive	independent	goal-oriented

Many of the women may have circled these particular adjectives because they represent socially desirable traits in our society. These values represent relationship and community, the two dominant aspects of women's social roles in our society.

The least common perceptions included:

courageous	moderate	gutsy	ordered	
humble	bold	reserved	fulfilled	liberal

The women may not have identified, or may not have reported their identification, with adjectives such as *courageous, gutsy,* and *bold* because such words are more stereotypically masculine traits. They may not have identified with adjectives like *liberal* and *moderate* because these words may suggest some type of political affiliation.

Interestingly, in follow-up interviews, self-identified courageous women, as a group, were found to be quite similar to women who did not identify themselves as courageous. This supported my premise that women who think of themselves as courageous may not comprise a large percentage of the population, but are a small group that has embraced the concept of courage as a tool for fulfillment in their lives.

Courageous women, like noncourageous women, rated themselves as:

intelligent open-minded honest happy independent

At the other end of the spectrum, both coura-

57

geous and noncourageous women circled these words less frequently:

ordered   liberal   reserved   moderate

Noncourageous women reported being more:
practical (27.4 percent versus 12.7 percent)
sensible (33.1 percent versus 14.1 percent)

Courageous women reported being more:
bold (12.7 percent versus 5.4 percent)
gutsy (18.3 percent versus 9.2 percent)
visionary (26.8 percent versus 11.0 percent)*

How did you define yourself? Was *courageous* one of your words? Whether courage was or was not one of your nine traits, the powerful three-step process that follows will reveal how to summon courage more and more into your daily life.

'A special thank you to Susan K. R. Adams for providing the quantitative analysis of the data from the survey. Ms. Adams holds a master's degree in Industrial and Organizational Psychology from the University of Colorado at Denver. Her research interests include the glass-ceiling phenomena and women's acquisition and effective use of influence and power in organizations.

PARTS TWO AND THREE

THREE-STEP PROCESS
FOR INTEGRATING COURAGE
Chapter Six

- **Self-Discovery**
- **Source Wheel**
- **Techniques**

STEP ONE
SELF-DISCOVERY
Chapter Seven

- **Conduct a self-audit**
- **Develop inner observer**
- **Identify issues and patterns**
- **Change habits**

STEP TWO
SOURCE WHEEL
Chapter Eight

- **Identify behaviors of courage**
- **Reframe issues and patterns**

STEP THREE
TECHNIQUES
Chapter Eight

- **Develop plan from Source Wheel**
- **Take specific actions**

CHAPTER SIX

MODELING THE
THREE-STEP PROCESS

There is plenty of courage among us
for the abstract, but not for the concrete.

Helen Keller

IMPLEMENTING COURAGE

Every woman possesses the potential for an interesting, engaging life, and implementing courage is
key to that kind of life. Within each of us lies the
ability to live with courage, yet an inner creation is
often required to reclaim this forgotten virtue. Such
a change of heart allows women to discern their
own character so they not only enjoy a good life for
themselves, but can bring out their highest human
qualities, reshaping negative circumstances to serve
their families, their community, and their country.
You, too, can use the Three-Step Process to discover
and claim your own courage. The opportunity to integrate courage is encountered not just in physically
dangerous situations, but in almost every aspect of
life. I selected the creative and recreational examples of art and golf.

THE THREE-STEP PROCESS IN AN ART CLASS

Art teachers know that students show up to class the
first day with preconceived purposes, along with
fears, self-doubt, confusion, flaws, and even exag-

gerated self-confidence about their artistic abilities. One savvy art teacher designed an exercise to break down the attitudes of his adult students. He used a three-step process that reframed traditional ways of instructing and opening his students to new insights. His three-step process parallels the three steps you take to integrate courage into your life.

Step One (Self-Discovery): The teacher tells the students to draw circles on the paper in front of them. They are miffed at this instruction. Wondering what drawing circles has to do with drawing a human figure. They ask, "Do I draw big circles, small circles, tight circles, one circle or many?"

The instructor coaches them by saying, "Enjoy for the moment drawing circles! Let yourself open up to a new process." The purpose is to eliminate the students' attitudes about art, particularly about drawing the nude figure. It is no easy task to get old ideas out of their heads so that they are no longer stuck in their perceptions about drawing. Students who observe closely become aware of their own thought patterns—and gain the insight that their thoughts expose similar patterns in their lives.

Then the teacher tells them to draw the nude using circles. Once again, the participants question the exercise. They wonder why circles would be used to draw a human figure. The students create excuses and justifications for staying inhibited, limited, and closed to new approaches and ideas.

Step Two (Source Wheel): Next, the teacher directs them to look closely at their nude drawings. He pushes by asking, "What part of the nude's body did you not draw?" The students notice and answer: the hands, the feet, the head, buttocks, or whatever. This process guides each student's awareness about what intimidates him or her most about drawing the human figure and what needs to be learned and applied to effectively draw a complete nude figure.

Step Three (Techniques): The instructor tells the students to go to the files or books that focus on the omitted part and find an exercise that illustrates the techniques to, say, draw a model's hands. They now work on that exercise.

Through this process students learn to appreciate the value of facing unfamiliar tasks. It requires them to accept new potential outcomes, and they begin to see beyond their preconceptions. As seekers, they acquire new characteristics and discover additional interesting results, such as a positive attitude, increased self-esteem, or a diminished fear of failure. They evolve!

Women who apply this same procedure to activities in their lives can overcome their fear of change and discover a simple truth. What lies at the center (*cor*) is courage, a primary source of growth. A journey of self-discovery reframes the patterns of the past and uncovers new perspectives. Once this happens, powerful capabilities emerge that were previously only dreamed of or intuitively known—but never expected or realized.

A journey of self-discovery reframes the patterns of the past and uncovers new perspectives.

A THREE-STEP PROCESS TO IMPROVE GOLF

In March 1999, Susan Morgan wrote an article entitled "Par Excellence" for *Mirabella* about a five-day workshop called "Golf in the Kingdom: An Exploration of the Deeper Game" at the Esalen Institute in Big Sur, California.

This approach to improving one's golf game was developed in 1992 by Steve Cohen, an Esalen Gestalt-therapy practitioner and self-described golf hacker. The workshop echoes the philosophy of Esalen cofounder Michael Murphy, who wrote about golfer Shivas Irons in his cult-classic novel *Golf in the Kingdom*. The method used in the workshop parallels the Three-Step Process used to integrate courage into one's life.

Step One (Self-Discovery): The participants have questions before they arrive, including, "Do I bring my clubs?" and "Is the workshop only for experienced golfers?" They quickly learn that they need no clubs or golf balls at the first session. Instead, they talk about what they want from the game of golf, such as "ultimate happiness," "to crush an opponent," "to revel in the great outdoors," "to no longer be a golf widow," and "to enjoy a good game without breaking my bones." In their discussions, they explore fear, trust, self-esteem, and the desire to achieve. The leader jots these comments down on a flip chart for future reference.

Group members do some yoga stretches and visualization exercises to instill awareness. Then they are told to look at the person sitting opposite them and, noting what they observe, to complete the sentence, "I see—."

How does this relate to golf and implementing courage? The exercise reveals how people express preconceived notions in the way they view others. The leader wants these preconceptions and assumptions stripped away.

Next, the participants do the same exercise with their predetermined ideas about golf. They are asked to close their eyes and "go on interior journeys to familiar golf courses, where they encounter their pasts populated by ex-spouses, hated teachers, and elderly parents." Dismantling self-consciousness and competitive urges, participants recognize how common such unfounded preconceptions can be. Sensing their common problem, they start to trust each other, shifting to a supportive frame of mind rather than a competitive one.

Step Two (Source Wheel): Gradually, the participants move on to playing the game. They go to a four-hole makeshift pitch-and-putt course overlooking the ocean. Filled with a new awareness of the golf game as a metaphor for certain aspects of their lives, some speak up about the glory of the experience. Some let go of their desire to be perfect in everything they do. Others may find the process too risky for comfort. Nonetheless, they are able to look at the quality of their responses to their life experiences.

Step Three (Techniques): Using a unique scoring system, the golfers think about and quantify how each hole fulfills what they desire from golf. They look at how they examine the issues they uncovered in Step One. Each day, the golf experience expands their awareness as they watch the balls fly off into the Pacific Ocean, carrying with them old expectations.

The weeklong workshop ends with a scramble match played in a newly awakened purity of spirit. The players set aside personal agendas and the desire to win. The delightful day opens with everyone hollering with joy. They meditate and visualize the golf course. The idea that people love and support them lingers in their minds. They know it's true— they've been experiencing it all week. The workshop has been a magnificent experience with or without golf clubs.

While the golfers learn from this self-exploration,

65

our own self-determined life stories and expectations may hold us in a state of stagnation. We seek mirrors of what we determine to be the essence of our personal life stories, such as "I am unworthy of success." We live and die in the mirrors we create for ourselves on our journeys.

We live and die in the mirrors we create for ourselves on our journeys.

The process calls for hard work—seeing yourself as you really are, not as you imagine. The journey also requires seeing problems as opportunities for growth. A vital first step to build character—to build a reservoir of courage—is to realize the consequences of your thoughts, words, and deeds.

Using the Three-Step Process for Integrating Courage, every woman can reveal the rainbow of her life, both past and present. She can examine each shade and hue determined by the memories, attitudes, beliefs, and influences that make up her subconscious mind. She can observe the design that the rainbow forms and can identify lifelong patterns.

There is joy in the result. When you define yourself as courageous, you begin to act differently. By integrating the attributes of courage, you have a method to guide you as you start anew on your journey, step by step.

STEP ONE

SELF-DISCOVERY

Chapter Seven

- **Conduct a self-audit**

- **Develop inner observer**

- **Identify issues and patterns**

- **Change habits**

SELF-DISCOVERY

To acquire knowledge, one must study;
but to acquire wisdom, one must observe.

Marilyn vos Savant

KNOW THYSELF

Women's magazines use quizzes to entice women to gain new insights: "Twenty questions to find your best type of man." "Are you raising your children to be kind?" "Take this quiz to determine if you have charisma." "Do you make your lover feel loved?"

While it is fun to take quizzes, we usually settle for only a few amusing tugs at our psyches and we keep living the same unproductive patterns and producing the same outcomes. Yet if we take to heart the ancient Greek axiom, *know thyself,* we realize where the journey must begin.

Knowing ourselves at a deeper level tests the boundaries of our personalities and pushes our growth beyond the immediate comfort zone. Achieving self-awareness is difficult. Such a quest forces us to peel back the protective layers of emotion that have built up over the years. Yet that is what we must do if we are to expand our boundaries and allow for new choices.

Begin your journey by conducting a self-audit. You may find the process frustrating or feel it is unsafe. You may be afraid that your life will be changed by your answers. That is exactly what happened to me while writing this book. During the early stages, I became very frustrated. I often lost my courage. At times, I realized I was not listening, not looking, or simply not being aware. I actually became angry and admonished myself, "Sandra, you're a trainer. Design a training program to reveal your stories of courage."

By doing a self-audit, I began to weave together the fabric of my courageous connections at a deep level. Bits and pieces came together explaining why I live in a certain way. I started by writing down the aspects of my life that I perceived as involving courage. Upon review, I realized courage was actually etched onto every pane of my life. Drawing from my *cor* became my guide.

Upon review, I realized courage was actually etched onto every pane of my life.

GOING IN BEFORE GOING OUT

To begin your self-discovery, randomly write down over the course of a week or a month all the memorable stepping stones in your life. These experiences might be either joyful or painful. For example, becoming pregnant again soon after a first child is born may be bad timing, but not bad news. List on page 72 (Stepping Stones in My Life) all the mishaps, disappointments, challenges, changes, even victories. Include the emotional as well as the physical ordeals. Make sure you don't judge yourself or the events as good or bad or right or wrong. You are simply listing your personal perceptions of events that have had an impact on your life. List even the childhood ones you don't remember but were told about by older people. Let the memories bubble to consciousness as this process slowly brews, and then place the events in sequential order starting with your youngest years up to today.

This "going in before going out" approach to personal and interpersonal effectiveness helps you to start with the most inside part of the self. This blueprint for self-observation unveils your past character, motives, projections, and beliefs. Learning about your deepest self can free you from being stuck in the mud of old vices. It can yank you out of the muck into new awareness. This new awareness will help you develop new virtues and ways of being in the world. The idea is to develop the ability to observe your motivations and actions at the same time you are living life. This mindfulness calls for a heightened consciousness on all levels at once.

The idea is to develop the ability to observe your motivations and actions at the same time you are living life.

Stepping Stones in My Life

INNER OBSERVER

Your inner observer is the part of yourself that stands back from the busy, reactive side and objectively observes what is going on. Learning to listen to your observer can assist you in more accurately reading a situation so that you know how to be effective. The inner observer helps you identify old recurring patterns and beliefs that hold you back.

As you list the experiences in your life, you will see how your inner observer remains on conscious duty, noticing thoughts, feelings, relationships, purpose, motivation, and passion. Your observer reveals how you choose to see the world and what action and reaction patterns you habitually follow. This awareness is vital to overcoming negative and unwanted patterns—and to reinforcing positive and beneficial patterns.

Your observer reveals how you choose to see the world and what action and reaction patterns you habitually follow.

IDENTIFYING CURRENT PATTERNS

Once you have compiled your list of life events, write down one issue, problem, or conflict that is currently bothering you. The next step is to use the personal microscope of "Why?" and "What?" questions to unravel the pattern and expose the issue at its core.

The magic of "Why?" and "What?" questions have always intrigued me. They offer an insightful, often surprising, way to find the meanings we have assigned to events. Review the experiences you wrote down on the previous page. The following questions can help ferret out patterns of meaning:

- What do I avoid?
- What is my underlying motivation?
- What inhibits me?
- What gives me energy?

73

- Why do I respond the way I do?
- Why do I feel afraid?
- Why don't I go after what I say is important?
- Why don't I take action when I should?
- Why don't I answer my own "Why?" questions?

When you uncover a pattern, you may notice that you have at some time made a vow designed to cope with that pattern. For example, you may have vowed that from now on you would never trust anyone, never be angry, never be ordinary, never let your guard down, or never give up control. The pattern reveals how you carry the past into the present.

You may have oriented your life around avoiding this pattern. Understanding avoidance is the key here. What were (and are) the advantages of having this vow in your life? What will be the benefits of keeping it operating? It takes courage to face and overcome your habitual patterns. The process may encounter resistance, and resistance is the trap that prevents you from being the architect of your destiny.

You will only change when the pain of staying in the old pattern is greater than the pain of change.

But "Why?" and "What?" questions only take you so far. Now ask the question "How?" to actually effect a change. How do I continually re-create, and thus relive, the past? How do I continue wounding myself? Mustering the motivation to change often involves facing some painful circumstance. You will only change when the pain of staying in the old pattern is greater than the pain of change. Then you will begin the journey of self-knowledge and transformation.

My strongest behavior pattern has been avoiding vulnerability. (Revealing vulnerability is one of the twelve Behaviors of Courage that will be discussed in the next chapter.) I have often vowed, "From now on, never look weak, never be irresponsible, never be dependent on anyone, never be without choices, never want for anything, never be poor, and never ask for help."

When I moved, only to be unexpectedly dumped by the man I was to marry, I became especially vulnerable. To start my business and make friends, I had to ask for help. I was surprised when people stepped forward to help me, especially because giving, for me, had always been easier than receiving. I realized how much I needed people in my life and how much they wanted to lend a hand. Through this process, I saw that my pattern of avoiding vulnerability matched my beliefs: "Never trust anyone. Never succumb to someone else's belief system. Never totally unite. Never believe anyone could be accountable."

I still cry the tears of lost courage as I remember the persuasiveness of this pattern that kept me from fully living my life and experiencing the wonder of family and friends. I find that the pattern still has a strong hold on my life. Recalling and reading about my own pain is still difficult, although I have worked, and continue to work, to change the pattern of behavior that keeps me stuck in the past.

CHANGING YOUR HABITS

Often when you feel you are in a trap, no alternatives appear to exist. But as your inner observer matures and redefines everyday actions as courageous, you will develop a sharpened awareness of options. You will have the strength to choose one of those alternatives. And you will have formed a new and valuable habit—shaping your own life.

According to Stephen Covey, author of *The 7*

Habits of Highly Effective People, the process of making new habits involves three components: knowledge, desire, and skill. Knowledge increases as our awareness of our behavior extends our ability to design new habits and skills. Eventually, the investment in courage increases, giving the new habit a toehold in the psyche.

Desire grounds courage in its proper place. Many *Desire* women have experienced fleeting moments of *grounds* strength, faith, or conviction in extraordinary cir- *courage in its* cumstances. However, feelings of fear or the author- *proper place.* itative voices of old tapes playing in our heads may soon paralyze us. We forget how to draw upon and claim our voice of courage. When the extraordinary circumstance vanishes, we may return to our original ways of viewing the world.

Nevertheless, the possibility of expressing courage is not lost. Rather, it is a question of remembering a choice that may temporarily have been forgotten. We forget to draw upon our often untapped but ongoing reservoir of courage. Merely calling upon your courage will unleash your sense of self-worth.

Part Three (Chapter Eight) describes the twelve Behaviors of Courage and relates the real-life stories of women who have drawn upon the behaviors noted on the Source Wheel (see page 86). The anecdotes portray how contemporary women used their courage to transform their lives. The blueprint for growth identifies and provides the inspiration to embrace courageous attitudes and actions. These courageous women explored the unknown, created change, confronted abuse, embraced faith, conquered fear of failure, left unhappy relationships, 76 and chose their own paths.

PART THREE

TRANSFORMATION

TRANSFORMATION

PUTTING YOUR LIFE ON A POSITIVE PATH

I admire the courage of the women I interviewed over the years of writing this book. We cried together as they shared their stories of struggle, conflict, joy, and fulfillment. These women embody what Hemingway called "grace under pressure." In almost every case, women facing dilemmas overcame what seemed at the time insurmountable obstacles and drew from inner reservoirs of courage. Each woman made a conscious choice to make her world better and, in doing so, transformed her life. These stories highlight techniques for integrating courage into any situation and specific actions that any woman can take when confronted with a setback.

Like these women, I began to reflect on the times in my own life when I faced situations that required me, one more time, to use courage to make necessary changes. The choices I made brought me to where I am today. I realize that my choices collectively affected every aspect of myself and the world around me. I have used the word *transformation* to capture the insights of the new awareness of self.

I have come a good distance on my own yellow brick road like Dorothy's road to Oz, paved by my choices. Every woman has a little of Dorothy in her. No matter how tough life may be, action springs from making conscious choices. The opportunity to choose is always there, and finding the courage to make a good choice is paramount if you are to transform your life for the better.

The opportunity to choose is always there, and finding the courage to make a good choice is paramount . . .

79

Self-deception runs deep in human nature. Women wear many masks for many different situations, and we must be clear that the choices we make are based on our real selves and not the masks we wear. If we are not careful, our choices may be based on false assumptions. For example, you may falsely assume that you are not competent. The resulting behavior can lead you down the wrong path. A clear and deeply felt intention to get rid of the masks is important.

The journey of this book is to *en*courage every woman to make the choice to dispel false limitations, to draft a new perception of her life. Confident women have the power to do so. This book also aims to foster a new awareness of courage through language and a reclaiming of courage through conscious choice. The Roman poet Ovid said, "Courage conquers all things." Understanding this simple truth is the key to achieving transformation.

"Courage conquers all things."

STEP TWO
SOURCE WHEEL

Chapter Eight

- **Identify behaviors of courage**

- **Reframe issues and patterns**

STEP THREE
TECHNIQUES

Chapter Eight

- **Develop plan from Source Wheel**

- **Take specific actions**

BEHAVIORS OF COURAGE

You gain strength, courage and confidence
by every experience in which you really stop
to look fear in the face . . . You must do the thing
which you think you cannot do.

Eleanor Roosevelt

STEP-BY-STEP ACTION

The courageous women depicted in the following pages share heartrending stories of adjustments in their lives. They reveal techniques to tap into their reservoirs of courage, and the benefit of living more fully with courage. I hope they will be an inspiration to you as much as they have been to me.

Making changes is not easy. Just mention change and there is an instant aversion to the word, even to the idea. Change can be a fearsome concept, because often it is difficult to observe. Giant leaps are seldom associated with change; it occurs in incremental steps.

Working to change our consciousness is not easy. I have often questioned the popular elementary school drug education program (DARE) tenet, "Just say no." A TV program revealed, sadly, that the program has had little success. Just saying no did not keep kids off drugs. I realized I could not coax a woman by saying, "Just use courage!" Courage will not magically appear to support someone; it requires effort.

Perhaps women have been asleep to the truth that they have always been courageous. Though every woman's life is replete with instances of profound courage, we have been conditioned to believe that we are the "less significant" sex. Our consciousness of our courage has remained dormant. Now we must waken and claim our rightful heritage.

First, it is critical to acknowledge the courage in all of us. Second, each of us must undergo a personal internal change by altering our thought patterns about our own life. Recognizing the power of courage makes all the difference. Courage is a tool expressed from the heart—a tool used to approach life's dilemmas. Even the slightest internal change causes a reaction in our external world. By integrating courage in our hearts and spirits day by day, we change our lives.

Courage is a tool expressed from the heart—a tool used to approach life's dilemmas.

To change a situation you must change yourself. To change yourself, you may first have to change your perspective about the role of courage in women's everyday experiences. Is courage the fuel for your engine?

There is a tendency for family dynamics to be passed on through the generations. When a woman in a family structure demonstrates courage in a positive way, it affects many lives, both in the present and into the future. Visualizing yourself in harmony with courage builds positive relationships. Even when you feel anxious about change, do not let such feelings rob you of your courage. With courage comes transformation. Be willing to participate in the process. Such openness provides fresh insight into every challenge.

COURAGE COMES FROM WITHIN

Courage manifests itself in many forms, yet most women do not detect courage in themselves. Why? Perhaps women have been conditioned to believe that their everyday lives are ordinary and present very little challenge. Women naturally build relationships, take care of the home, bear and raise children, build careers, and support community goals. Contrary to popular belief, these acts are extraordinary. They require surmounting some of life's most difficult challenges, and they prove that courage is an integral part of every woman's life.

Women interviewed for this book did more than just pay lip service to courage. They used courage in their daily lives as well as when they encountered serious risks. Often their courage took on heroic qualities that displayed great strength and determination. By calling on the Behaviors of Courage, they were able to stand alone when necessary to defend their values.

Perhaps women have been conditioned to believe that their everyday lives are ordinary and present very little challenge.

Source Wheel
Behaviors of Courage

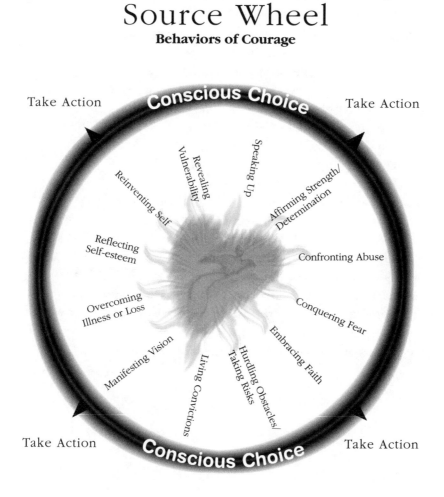

Take Action

Conscious Choice

Take Action

Speaking Up

Revealing Vulnerability

Reinventing Self

Affirming Strength/ Determination

Reflecting Self-esteem

Confronting Abuse

Overcoming Illness or Loss

Conquering Fear

Manifesting Vision

Embracing Faith

Hurdling Obstacles/ Taking Risks

Living Convictions

Take Action

Conscious Choice

Take Action

Affirming Strength and Determination

Cautious, careful people, always casting
about to preserve their reputations . . .
can never effect a reform.

Susan B. Anthony

Taking a Look at Yourself

When you fail to tackle a challenge, your lack of resolve may be fueled by questions such as: Am I smart enough? Am I strong enough? Am I prepared? What will people think?

Each woman interviewed for this book responded to a survey form (see Research and Survey Results, page 56) and chose the nine behaviors that she felt applied to her from a list of thirty-six words. Several of the respondents circled the word *determination.* Though many felt strength was required to handle tough situations, several commented it was easier to think of one's self as strong rather than courageous. They felt the word *courage* could only be used to describe a person with a heroic uniqueness, not an average person living an ordinary life. One woman confessed she had to struggle with her low self-esteem in order to recognize that she was courageous. She felt more comfortable just saying, "I am a strong person." After all, *courageous* is a powerful adjective to attribute to one's self! A few of the women found it easier to say they had tenacity. But, persistence is an inherent part of courage.

. . . persistence is an inherent part of courage.

Rebecca felt her older sister was always the

courageous one in the family because she was strong and determined in her approach to life. She noticed how her sister would speak up and hold her ground when challenged. Rebecca considered herself weak and a follower.

Rebecca discovered her courage around the age of forty-five, when people began to tell her she was courageous for enduring a horrible and humiliating divorce, then building a new life. Now in her fifties, she understands why these actions were seen as courageous. "I began to wonder," she says "where this strength came from."

What took courage for Rebecca was to ask herself honestly: What are my strengths, and what are my weaknesses? How do I need to change, and what do I need to do? "It would have been easier," she admitted, "to ignore and stuff the problems away somewhere."

". . . courage is light in utter darkness, a journey from loneliness to solitude and, once again, to laughter."

On the survey form, Rebecca circled *courageous* as one of nine words that described her. "For me, courage is light in utter darkness, a journey from loneliness to solitude and, once again, to laughter. Courage is listening to your heart, trusting in your resilience to bounce back, and not being afraid to start over when necessary." Rebecca's insight triggered the memory of a sentence in the Bible, 1 Chron. 28:20, "Be strong and of good courage, and act. Do not be afraid or dismayed; for the Lord God, my God, is with you. He will not fail you or forsake you."

For Corinne, courage meant "facing reality and having the strength to follow through with the right actions." It was obvious to her that it took different degrees of courage to handle different types of problems.

One of the pillars of courage is an unwillingness

to be defeated. Many of the women felt it easier to recognize courage in other women than to see it in themselves. Donna commented, "I don't think a lot of women look deeply enough into themselves for their courage. My definition of courage is the ability to do anything you want to do, perhaps something you've never done before, and finding the strength to do it."

Many of the women felt it easier to recognize courage in other women than to see it in themselves.

Karen: Affirming Strength and Determination

Moving Forward

When Karen filled out the survey she chose strong words to describe herself: *bold, determined, active,* and *risk-taking.* When I met her I saw that her earnest demeanor mirrored her determination to move forward. She answered my questions in crisp, clear sentences. Her desk revealed a multitasking person who could always squeeze in one more project. She seemed able to handle whatever needed to be done. But for Karen, these responsibilities were easy. "Nothing has been as difficult as almost losing my husband to cancer," she confesses, "even the death of my father. I drew on my internal courage to survive during that painful time."

Karen's thirty-five-year-old husband was diagnosed with lung cancer in 1990. She pondered all the normal and scary questions: Would he live? Would she be left by herself to raise her boys? How could she take care of her children and her ailing husband while working full-time and traveling for business?

Karen vowed she would do whatever was necessary to save her family's future. Even though her income was crucial to their financial stability, Karen took three weeks off from work to shuttle her husband back and forth to the hospital and to help him through those early weeks.

His right lung was removed during his first hospitalization. He endured chemotherapy, radiation therapy and seven subsequent hospital visits. Karen felt her only option was to hold her family together—to put one foot in front of the other every day. She recalled, "I would ask myself: What kind of courage am I going to need today?" Collapsing was not an option.

She enrolled her children in a cancer-victim's support group and informed their teachers about what they were going through. She resumed working every day, and after work she helped her husband overcome a variety of fears he had never experienced. Karen says, "I pushed him to go on walks, swim, and to complete his black belt in Tae Kwon Do."

I telephoned Karen the summer after our first interview. She told me her husband's cancer was still in remission, but though he was doing well it had not been an easy year. Karen said, "On top of everything else, my father was diagnosed in February with a malignant, fast growing cancer. By the end of March the doctors performed surgery." Knowing that her father did not have much time, she traveled back and forth across the country to offer emotional support in his recovery from surgery.

Karen felt enormous pressure to balance her work as a sales manager for an international company, write papers for graduate school, and attend to her husband and two sons while providing comfort to her father. Within a few weeks of his surgery, Karen's father passed away. She recalls, "It was very difficult to meet his wish to die at home, but we were able to accommodate his need by getting a hospital bed and having hospice care. He died at home. I miss him."

I admired Karen's unusual perseverance in facing the illnesses in her family. Her secret was breaking the task into little manageable parts and tackling one piece at a time. "I believe that courage is the ability to do what needs to be done in spite of difficult circumstances. I do what I need to do to keep myself and my family going."

Karen's husband just completed his ninth cancer-free year. She smiled as she added happily. "The kids still have their dad."

". . . courage is the ability to do what needs to be done in spite of difficult circumstances."

HOW KAREN TAPS INTO HER RESERVOIR OF COURAGE TO AFFIRM STRENGTH AND DETERMINATION:

- Do your best—no one expects perfection.
- Practice what is morally right.
- Never believe the situation is impossible.
- Continue to put one foot in front of the other. If you are immobile, you lose opportunities to use courage.
- Each day ask questions about what needs to be done.
- Make a plan, decide what to do next, and complete the task.
- Evaluate the resources available to you and utilize them.
- Maintain supportive friendships and, when possible, get a sitter.
- Take time for reflection. Draw on your courage by looking inward.
- Believe you can do whatever it takes without collapsing.

- Develop an internal evaluation system by asking: Am I doing the right thing? Am I on the right path? "Yes" answers strengthen your resolve.
- Read inspiring books such as *Chicken Soup for the Soul, One Minute for Yourself,* and *Gung Ho!: Turn on the People in Any Organization.*

"If you believe that you are courageous, you will act courageously."

Courage is a part of Karen's core self. It gave her the strength to cope with her husband's illness and the determination to move forward. She feels that identifying her actions as courageous has helped her discover a deep reservoir of courage within herself, which continues to expand as she faces new challenges in her life. "If you believe that you are courageous, you will act courageously. Women cannot allow courage to be solely a male attribute. After all, it's women who ultimately make the tough decisions."

Confronting Abuse

There are many ways of breaking a heart.
Stories are full of hearts broken by love, but
what really breaks a heart is taking away its
dream—whatever that dream might be.

Pearl S. Buck

SEXUAL ABUSE

Abuse breaks hearts by stealing dreams. Abused women develop mechanisms for blocking or distorting the truth. Yet many of the abused women interviewed for this book drew on their courage to put the abuse behind them.

The phrase "rule of thumb" is used in everyday conversation. It originated from the medieval common law, which gave a husband the right to beat his wife as long as the stick he used was "no thicker than his thumb." Just as this phrase has been innocently integrated into the English language, violence against women has been quietly tolerated as a part of American society. As long as abuse is tolerated, a society cannot evolve as a nation or a people.

Caroline Myss states in her book *Anatomy of the Spirit*, "Rape and incest of an energy field are motivated by the desire to cripple a person's ability to be independent and thrive outside the control of another person. Most of the time [these people] were constantly criticized about their physical appearance, their professional skills, ambitions, and accomplishments. In effect, they were 'raped' of their personal power needed for health and success."

Many women seem ready to believe messages of belittlement. If you are one who has followed this pattern, you probably hold a distorted image of yourself, and your identity no longer accurately reflects your true self. Your true self has been lost.

Having someone exercise power over you that is against your will has a major impact on your development. Women are encouraged to look sexy, dress sexy, and be sexy, yet women who are raped are blamed for looking, dressing, or being too sexy.

Abuse breaks hearts by stealing dreams.

Women are placed in a no-win situation. Rape is not an act of sexual intention; it is an abuse of power in which a women becomes the victim of a man who is obsessed with powerlessness. The rapist uses physical aggression and intimidation to assuage his inadequate feelings.

Jan: Confronting Abuse

From Humiliation to Pride in Identity

Jan did not seem to be courageous when she was a young child. Though pretty, she was shy and not very outgoing. She waited until she was an adult to claim courage as an attribute.

Raised a Catholic and married at the age of eighteen, she believed that marriage vows were sacred. She did not realize the potential for abuse until one year into her marriage. She stated, "Before Aaron was born, I could please my husband sexually." But after she became a mother, Jan's husband would rape her if she refused his sexual advances.

One time, after the birth of their third child, the sexual abuse was so severe she could barely walk. The bruising and swelling required a visit to the doctor, and revealed her abuse.

"I remember sitting in the waiting room of the doctor's office with ice packs between my legs," she recalls. "I used ice packs for three days along with prescription painkillers. I had given away my self-esteem in my marriage." When the doctor asked what happened, Jan could not answer. That was the turning point. She swore she would never allow herself to be abused again—marital rape was over.

Two-and-a-half months after that life-changing incident, Jan left her husband to start her life over with her children. She had endured eight years of abuse. She says, "I could not live like that anymore. I knew I would rather be alone for the rest of my life." She didn't want to raise her children in a loveless home. Concerned that her sons would grow up to treat women the way her husband treated her, she also worried that her daughter would marry an abusive man. "My children watched their mother be treated horribly by their father. There was no positive role model of a marriage. What took the most courage was taking my kids away from their dad. That was tough!" Jan exclaims. She rented a U-Haul truck and moved across the country with no friends or family. But she has no regrets. "Once I found the courage to reinvent myself, to start a new life, I never wanted anyone to take that away. I had always been someone's wife or someone's mother, but never just me. This was a whole new experience for me."

Jan's fears about being alone or thinking no one would love her or her children vanished in her new life. She found joy in being single. With confidence came peace of mind. Finding a new partner was not a priority. Her newfound independence outweighed her fears. "When you're afraid to do something, you need to look deep inside yourself. You need to do what feels right, even if others disagree. In the end, if you have the courage to leave an abuser, the rewards will be worth it. A little bit of courage can propel a woman to a new level of action. I knew I had done something right when my son said, 'Mom, at first I wasn't happy that you left Dad, but I think we're much better off now without him.' "

Jan believes everyone has the power to make the right choices when faced with a crisis. Some crises are small, such as running out of gas in the car.

"When you're afraid to do something, you need to look deep inside yourself."

95

Others are big, such as divorce or physical abuse. Jan says, "At some point, a woman will say to herself, 'I have a choice. I can either crawl on my hands and knees, or I can get up and dust myself off and walk away.' I chose to pick myself up. In the end I found happiness."

At the close of the interview, Jan admitted that it took great courage for her to remarry. It required her to be vulnerable, and she had to draw on her resources of courage to make that commitment. Her courage paid off. Abuse no longer is a factor in her life, depleting her life force. Keeping boundaries of your physical body, she feels, is critical to support a sense of self and of power.

Raised to believe that you do not quit, and you do not break up a family, she felt she would be a failure in the eyes of her family and friends if she left her husband.

"When marital rape is involved, all the scars are inside. It's not like seeing bruises on the outside. There's no real proof. I didn't tell anyone because I didn't believe anyone would believe me." She rationalized by saying to herself, "Oh, well, it only happens occasionally." Jan recalls, "During the good days, I told myself we were turning a corner."

Behind every abusive event, no matter how painful, an opportunity for growth occurs.

As Jan's story illustrates, the way you feel about yourself determines the quality of your life. It affects your work, relationships, and spiritual growth. You attract relationships that reflect and reinforce your self-image. Recognize demeaning early experiences or patterns and deal with them. Healing painful memories, then releasing them, exercises personal power and strengthens courage. Behind every abusive event, no matter how painful, an opportunity for growth occurs. Eventually, as you let go of your emotional history, healing begins. Most abused women have a hidden intuition that they should not accept the abuse they are suffering. If a woman has the courage to follow that intuition, personal power can be reclaimed.

Jan suffered gross indignities, fear, deprivation of spirit, and loss of self at the hands of her abuser. Deep personal insights became possible when she gained the courage to put aside an entire belief system and embrace the unknown.

Eventually, Jan's family's belief system did not matter. She decided she did not deserve to live in an abusive relationship. She had to save herself and her children. Today, at thirty-four, Jan is a working mom with a successful second marriage and she feels she is courageous every day.

A woman learns through situations what her level of internal strength may be, and then determines how to pull her courage out of her heart. Jan concluded, "I am the most confident person. I can do anything. I can be whatever I want to be. I can make it in this world!"

HOW JAN TAPS INTO HER RESERVOIR OF COURAGE TO CONFRONT ABUSE:

- Demand to be treated with respect.
- Learn courage by observing courageous people.
- Think positively about your capabilities. Be an optimist.
- Build self-esteem by letting go of negative feelings and old patterns.
- Be independent. Know you can take care of yourself.
- Believe that you have a choice.
- Keep control of your life.
- Experience and live in peace.

Jan believes that the key to finding courage is self-esteem. "If you have self-esteem, you'll get back up when you're knocked down." It took courage for Jan to face the fears she carried around for years. She feels if you know deep inside that you are worth something, then you can find the courage to face anything. "The biggest benefit of courage was finding my independence. I have control over my life. My life doesn't depend on me making somebody else happy. I now focus on making myself happy, which in turn, makes me a better wife, a better mom, and a better human being."

Conquering Fear

Real courage is when you know you're licked
before you begin, but you begin anyway
and see it through no matter what.

Harper Lee

ARE YOU LIVING IN THE SHADOW OF LOST OPPORTUNITIES?

Conquering fear prevents you from living in the shadow of lost opportunities. Until you begin to understand your fears, you cannot honestly assess your own strengths and weaknesses. Fears are a distorted view of yourself and your abilities. The process of self-exploration requires you to change your well-settled views of yourself and answer some uncomfortable questions: Am I afraid others will think I am incompetent? What do I fear might happen? Is my view of the situation realistic?

Conquering fear allows you to unearth your true self. Gavin de Becker reveals two key rules about fear in his book, *The Gift of Fear*. The first rule states: "The very fact that you fear something is solid evidence that it is not happening." Rule number two states: "What you fear is rarely what you think you fear—it is what you link to fear."

Fear is a signal that something might happen. Becker explains, "If it does happen, we stop fearing it and start to respond to it, manage it, surrender to it; or we start to fear the next outcome we predict might be coming."

"When you overcome your fear, you can see things from a different perspective," Gavin de Becker continued. "Facing the unknown is like sitting with your back to the warmth and security of a campfire. Cowboys have always known that they are safer sitting with their backs to the fire. Staring at the fire blinds you to the dangers that lurk in the darkness. If you face away from the flames, you can see danger approaching and take appropriate action. As you conquer your fear, you learn that it is more important to face the unknown than to compromise your courage. Compromise leads to self-doubt and even self-loathing. By facing your fears you are able to release them. As a result, you can seize every opportunity and live without regrets."

Conquering fear prevents you from living in the shadow of lost opportunities.

Bonnie: Conquering Fear

Doing What Is Uncomfortable

There are three kinds of fears. The smallest of these fears arises when you go to the dentist or see a police car in the rearview mirror. The second is felt deep inside. It represents rejection and being found a fraud. This fear causes you to feel abandoned and tells you, "I am not pretty enough, smart enough, or successful enough." Eventually such fears can cause disease (*dis*-ease), which erodes life's deepest meaning. The third type of fear is the greatest fear of all. This fear convinces you that you will never be loved authentically.

Bonnie's fear that she would never be loved started with her father's death when she was nine years old. The devastating loss made her feel alone and she has carried a fear of abandonment with her ever since.

The younger of two sisters, Bonnie identifies her courage with fear. With the death of her father in the 1950s, Bonnie's mother, at thirty-eight, became the head of the household and had to go to work for the first time. Becoming a latch-key kid, Bonnie was forced to be independent. She found herself eating alone in restaurants when other kids were going home for lunch. She feared she was not like the other kids. Bonnie says, "I was afraid to walk into a room and find that all the chairs were taken. I felt so noticeable. I was self-conscious and thought that I would not blend in as normal. I felt apart from the other kids."

To overcome her fear of not being accepted, Bonnie began imitating movie stars such as the stylish

> *"As you conquer your fear, you learn that it is more important to face the unknown than to compromise your courage."*

and independent Audrey Hepburn. She would imagine a scene from a movie in her head and try to act like the confident star. This assumption of courage made Bonnie feel strong and romantic about her aloneness. Her intriguing aura of competence soon attracted friends who provided the love she sought.

Now at age fifty-six, with a lion's mane of hair, Bonnie looks confident and courageous. She has a different perspective about courage. "When we say the word *courage* I think we have a picture in our mind of someone being very daring and taking enormous risks. But overcoming fear is a great act of courage. I think that without fear there is no such thing as courage. Courage is about being fearless enough to stand on your own and be your own person." Bonnie also feels courage is about pushing past fear in order to move through life, rather than being paralyzed in fear and simply existing. She continues, "To get past fear takes a conscious push. I don't think there's a measuring stick for courage because each case is different and personal. It's simply about doing what makes you uncomfortable, getting past it, and making it happen."

"Courage is about being fearless enough to stand on your own and be your own person."

As an adult, Bonnie is a paradox. She teeters between being an emotionally shy person and an insatiable extrovert. People sometimes are afraid to approach her because she looks too confident and inaccessible. Ironically, Bonnie now faces a new fear—fear of rejection for appearing too courageous.

Bonnie's paradox provided an opportunity to really use her courage. Even though Bonnie is dyslexic and failed her grammar classes in high school, she coauthored a book titled *How to Get a Man to Make a Commitment.* Using the book as a guide, Bonnie teaches dating and relationship workshops to help others who are seeking love. She says, "What takes courage is to teach from my own mistakes, to teach the truth, and to tell the truth about my own fearful experiences."

With each class, Bonnie knows she may have to endure a student's initial rejection of her story. When she tells the truth of her life, the participants may feel she is exposing too much. One student told her that she felt as if Bonnie were reading her mail because Bonnie was revealing so many truths about her. Many students are reluctant at first to acknowledge their fear. But Bonnie has learned that as she coaches her students, they, too, will learn to face their fears. "I have to step up to the plate when I really don't feel like it. I have to push myself into everything I do." In order to get results, Bonnie uncomfortably leads others through their own discomfort.

Offered her own talk-radio show, Bonnie was scared to death. She had no training to produce a two-hour radio show. Yet she said "yes" to the station's offer. She felt she could reach more people struggling with fears of rejection and lovelessness through a radio program than through her classes. Bonnie confesses, "I've been terrified of new experiences my whole life. Yet I know how important it is to say yes to opportunity. And I know that nothing will knock at my door unless I create motion. I always say to myself: 'What's the worst thing that can happen?' By asking that one question, I take the power out of the fear."

Bonnie continues her struggle with fear and courage. She believes one can only be courageous by overcoming fear. She has conquered the fears of her shy childhood while striving to get what we all want: to be loved and totally accepted for who we are.

HOW BONNIE TAPS INTO HER RESERVOIR OF COURAGE TO CONQUER FEAR:

- Ask yourself: What's the worst thing that can happen?
- Verbalize your fear.
- Invite others to become involved in your journey by telling your friends about your fears.
- Be introspective.
- Talk yourself into action.
- Observe how other people face their fears.
- Listen to the advice of others and hear the information without being defensive.
- Seek encouragement from others.

By sharing her story, Bonnie learned to be open about her frailties and vulnerabilities. By doing this, she not only faces her fears and moves forward, but she wins the affection of those to whom she entrusts her deepest feelings. Blessed with a terrific sense of humor and the ability to laugh at herself, Bonnie uses her courage to help others face the discomfort of their own fears. She believes that without fear, courage remains a shadow—a shadow that cannot be captured. "Courage is a road for me. My courage pushes me to be uncomfortable and make something happen."

. . . without fear, courage remains a shadow—a shadow that cannot be captured.

Embracing Faith

*Spiritual courage grows through our willingness
to keep on remembering, to keep on searching
for the sacred behind all the seemingly mundane
and even terrible facets of life.*

Joan Borysenko, Ph.D.,
Fire in the Soul

A POWER GREATER THAN OURSELVES

The ultimate source of courage comes from the
transcendent—a sense of faith in a power greater
than ourselves. As women begin redefining God to
include feminine qualities, they are able to use faith
to find the strength and determination to live a
courageous life.

It is not surprising to me that most of the women
I interviewed felt that courage involved believing in
and relying on divine authority. Though their faith
was based on no particular religion, many expressed a belief in God, "a power greater than one-
self."

*Belief in the
love and
power of God
gives them
courage.*

For the women who believe courage is about
faith or a belief in God, their creative thoughts are
sparked by the wisdom that God lives through
them. Their life is not limited to what they can perceive in the physical world. In the quiet of their
inner being, they experience a oneness with God.
This union allows them to face the challenges in
their world. Belief in the love and power of God
gives them courage. They recognize that this love

and power is available to everyone. For some, courage is having faith that they are divinely guided and protected.

Eva: **Embracing Faith**

The Glory of Belief

For Eva, courage and love go hand in hand. Both are part of her faith. She believes she was born with courage. She defines courage as overcoming the odds, doing something out of the ordinary, and, when necessary, standing alone. She believes that everyone is given a certain amount of courage. The difference lies in what you do with it.

Born in Berlin, Germany, she faced heavy burdens at a young age. Her parents were against the Hitler regime. But in 1938, at the age of ten she was expected to join the Hitler Youth. She explains, "I had almost no fear during the war. I was not afraid to die, nor did I think I would die. I felt God was watching over me. I think my whole childhood was geared toward having courage. The courage I had within me came from Him—from His love."

"The courage I had within me came from Him—from His love."

After the war, when Eva was twenty, she worked as a secretary and interpreter for the U.S Army. A Protestant, she fell in love with and married a Catholic American soldier. Eva's parents, who had sent her to a Lutheran church for her education and religious training, counseled her to remain Lutheran, as did her Lutheran confirmation teacher. When Eva chose to convert to Catholicism, her peers rejected her and her confirmation teacher demanded that Eva return the personal gift she had given her on her confirmation day.

Eva believed her conversion did not betray her

faith because Lutherans and Catholics prayed to the same God. She says, "There is only one God. He is the creator. What does it matter how I worship?" After her wedding in Germany, she and her husband moved to Hawaii. "My husband had the courage to take me to his family's plantation where eleven family members lived in a very tiny house. In Hawaii, at that time, there were no apartments, no homes that we could rent." The newlyweds moved into an enclosed porch attached to the house.

Eva not only had to adjust to a new country, living on an island, and being poor, but she also endured being shunned by the neighbors. The islanders rumored that German girls were hookers. People passing her in the street called her a whore. Fortunately, she had a wonderful and courageous mother-in-law. "She gave me the faith to stand up to the people who shunned me. She told me God knew my heart and who I was. Besides, I was her daughter, not daughter-in-law. She always told me that I should keep all the good I have within me and display it to others. That advice helped me endure the cold shoulders."

Eva's most painful hardship came when she gave birth to her first child. As a new convert, she placed her rosary beads over her bedpost to protect her during her delivery. She had a baby boy. But something was wrong. The doctor came into the hospital room. He told Eva, "Your son has cerebral palsy and this thing (pointing to the rosary) is not going to help you." Eva then put the rosary under her bed. The rosary did not protect Eva's firstborn from the affliction. The baby was given the last rites of the Catholic Church. The doctor told Eva to leave her severely palsied son in the hospital for treatment.

Eva remembered, "Three weeks later when I went to pick him up, I thought he might be better. He never was. That was a time when I questioned God's existence. I had a hard time understanding why it happened." Eva found herself asking: Am I being punished? What did I do to deserve this? Do I have enough faith?

Devastated, she and her husband put their son in a state hospital since there was no hope of him ever being cured. At one point, Eva contemplated suicide, even though she was taught that taking one's life was a sin. Desperately homesick for her homeland and weary of being poor, she fell into depression.

But Eva realized that such a desperate experience could either make or break her. An older friend helped her reclaim her courage, telling her, "Only special, courageous people are given these children. Other mothers would lie down and die or even do away with the child. God gives us these kinds of hardships to help us to grow in character."

"Then," Eva relates, "God began to talk to me. I would wait for His guidance. I remembered my childhood promise to Him to live my life in His service. And the feeling that God watches over me finally came back." She no longer thought about running in front of a bus. She set an example for the younger people in her new family.

Confident that God and faith pulled her out of her sorrow, Eva now relies on a poem titled "Footprints in the Sand" (Mary Stevenson) that she has hanging on her living room wall. That's all it takes for Eva to reconnect with her faith.

FOOTPRINTS IN THE SAND

*One night I dreamed I was walking along the beach
with the Lord.
Many scenes from my life flashed across the sky.
In each scene I noticed footprints in the sand.
Sometimes there were two sets of footprints.
Other times there were one set of footprints.
This bothered me because I noticed that during the
Low periods of my life
When I was suffering from anguish, sorrow, or defeat,
I could see only one set of footprints.
So I said to the Lord, "You promised me, Lord,
That if I followed you, you would walk with me always.
But I noticed that during the most trying periods of
my life
There have only been one set of prints in the sand.
Why, When I have needed you most,
You have not been there for me?" The Lord replied,
"The times when you have seen only one set of footprints
Is when I carried you."*

Mary Stevenson (1922–1999)

Eva added, "I want women to know that the feeling of courage is not guaranteed; there are lows in everyone's life. It's about falling down and getting up. To return to courage requires faith to remember the one set of footprints."

"I want women to know that the feeling of courage is not guaranteed . . ."

Now sixty-nine, Eva has eight children, twenty-two grandchildren, and nine great-grandchildren. She says, "Courage for me now is to help others seeking God. My aim is to encourage the young people to use their resources and be aware that they too can be courageous. I think I was born with a gift from God. Nothing has really changed over the years. With my courage, I don't have to struggle anymore."

Real courage trusts the invisible. We were born to recognize the glory of God that is within us. It is not just in some of us, it is in everyone. As we let our light shine, we give other people permission to do the same.

Real courage trusts the invisible.

How Eva Taps into Her Reservoir of Courage to Embrace Faith:

- Do what you love.
- Be a doer. Courage grows out of action.
- Do not hesitate when something has to be done.
- Create goals.
- Have a dream.
- Nurture hope.
- Believe God will help you.
- Follow your convictions.
- Be grateful and practice the Golden Rule.
- Think courage! Each step of courage makes the next step easier.
- Face the situation.
- In the end, stand alone if necessary.

All of Eva's courage is connected to love and faith. She believes that the gift of love comes from God. Certainly, God has many faces, just as courage has many faces. Eva can always turn to the Lord and ask, "What shall I do?"

"At my age courage is a way of life for me. It is always there, always available to be used. I believe that to live life to the fullest one has to have courage."

Hurdling Obstacles and Taking Risks

Courageous risks are life giving, they help you grow, make you brave and better than you think you are.

Joan L. Curcio

Is the Risk Worth It?

Rosa Parks had the courage to stand up for justice. This African-American woman boarded a bus to ride home from work on December 1, 1955, in Montgomery, Alabama. After she sat down, in the colored section, the bus driver asked her to give up her seat to a white man. The tired seamstress was fed up. She said "No." With that one word she helped launch the civil rights movement.

Courage is required to challenge the negatives in our daily lives. Women's roles have traditionally been viewed as "stopping at the front door." But, fortunately, today the important work of women is boundless. Bolstered by personal success, women are influencing their communities and transforming society. As more women gain the courage to change their daily lives, they can lead the whole world in the direction of peace and good.

Courage is required to challenge the negatives in our daily lives.

Many women do not realize that they are already working for a better planet. Perhaps you have written a letter to the local paper condemning current gun laws, marched to protest local pollution, or canvassed to raise money for AIDS research. These are

110

courageous, even risky, acts that make a difference in the world.

Courage is a vital energy that shields your heart and spirit and enables you to take risks to overcome obstacles. You risk the possibility that others will not agree with your actions. You may risk being called unfeminine, aggressive, or worse. Yet, risk-taking can be exciting and rewarding. It is a necessary part of growth and evolution. You can only follow your dreams if you take risks.

Courage is a vital energy that shields your heart and spirit and enables you to take risks to overcome obstacles.

Lila: Hurdling Obstacles and Taking Risks

Overcoming Old Barriers

Lila's first act of courage was to escape her drug- and alcohol-induced fog. In her thirties she was close to losing everything—her two-year-old twins, her marriage, and her financial stability.

Racked with feelings of guilt, she felt worse with each relapse. Each setback prompted her to immediately call her good friend and say, "I have used again." Her friend would promptly drive down from the mountains into the city where Lila lived, give Lila a hug and a flower, and tell her that she could whip her addiction. Her friend assured her that she could get clean and sober. Lila attended Alcoholics Anonymous meetings to gain the support she needed to prevent another relapse.

One time, after one more relapse, Lila again called her friend. As her friend approached the back door, Lila could see she was angry. There was no smile on her face, no loving look. Her friend marched through the back door thrust a handful of dead roses at her, slapped her across the face, and said, "Sit down!"

The friend then told Lila to write on four slips of paper something that was important to her. "I wrote down marriage, children, family, and siblings," Lila recalled. "Then my friend directed me to fold the four pieces of paper into quarters and put them in the middle of the table. She told me to take one piece of paper, unfold it, read it, and think about how I was destroying that precious thing. Then I was supposed to spit on it, rip it to shreds, throw it on the floor, and stomp it with my foot."

Lila did as she was directed with each piece of paper. Somehow, physically destroying those slips of paper, each representing something she loved, sparked the truth for her. She was destroying her life. Lila says, "This wasn't a game anymore. I was going to lose it all. I was going to die if I didn't get clean and sober." That was the beginning of her healing.

Lila made a conscious choice to put her addiction behind her. She believes she was born with courage, but that it had gotten lost somewhere along the way in her attempts to be accepted. It has only been in the last few years that she has become comfortable with the fact that she is courageous. Forced to make a life-or-death change, she realized she either had to get sober or lose everything that was important to her. She now affirms the truth and chooses to live her life differently.

. . . she realized she either had to get sober or lose everything that was important to her.

Lila recently celebrated ten years of sobriety. Now forty-two, she has her own company providing administrative services to nonprofit organizations. She is happily married with thirteen-year-old twins. "I would rather be hated for who I am, than liked for who I am not. I have finally stopped craving and struggling to fit in. I am beginning to embrace the idea that I am different and find the positive pieces to it, such as being willing to confront people and hold them accountable. In other words, to take a stand. For me, standing alone is the keystone of my courage." Finally comfortable with herself, Lila has turned her nonconformity into an asset.

Lila shared her philosophy of courage with her son and daughter. She told them to be true to themselves, regardless of what society dictates. "Hopefully, that attitude will make them courageous."

HOW LILA TAPS INTO HER RESERVOIR OF COURAGE TO HURDLE OBSTACLES:

- Give yourself permission to be different.
- Take action to turn your life around.
- Identify and nourish a "sound in your voice" that expresses hope.
- Believe that your behavior is a choice.
- Seek the support of others.
- Always ask: What is the worst thing that can happen?
- Remember that you would rather be hated for who you are, than liked for who you are not.

Lila now loves life more than ever. Because she is more self-confident, it is easier for her to make life-fulfilling choices. She believes she no longer has to "fit in" and is proud to follow her own path. "When I use courage, it doesn't take me as long to make decisions. I think of the word *courage* as I make decisions. I am no longer in the gutter digging out. I am willing to do more healthy activities, including traveling, joining a gym, and eating right. My choices today make my life better than I could have imagined."

"When I use courage, it doesn't take me as long to make decisions."

Living Convictions

With fame, notoriety, credibility—if you can't have the courage to stand up and speak out for what you truly believe in, then it means nothing.

Oprah Winfrey

THE COURAGE OF YOUR CONVICTIONS

Recognizing our history is important. Women have not always stood up for themselves. Authors like Louisa May Alcott began giving women and girls images of courageous women years before the political movements for equal rights. Her book *An Old-Fashioned Girl,* written in 1897, reveals the "coming woman," sculpted in clay. The main character in the book, Rebecca Jeffrey, is "skillfully wielding her tools" in a "queerly furnished room" occupied by her friend and roommate Bess, and two female visitors. They discuss what the beautiful female figure means to them. Rebecca tells them she will show them her "idea of the coming woman— see what a fine forehead, yet mouth is both firm and tender, as if it could say strong, wise things, as well as teach children and kiss babies . . . a woman is to stand alone, and help herself . . . strong-hearted, strong-souled, and strong-bodied; and that is why I made her larger than the miserable, pinched-up woman of our day. Strength and beauty must go together."

Gradually, a tidal wave of indignation was building. Women were finding the courage to assert their demands for equal rights. Alcott's character voiced her opinion about the future of women when she said, "Don't you think these broad shoulders can bear burdens without breaking down, these hands work well, these eyes see clearly, and these lips do something besides simper and gossip?"

Louisa May Alcott was one of the first authors to plant the seed that a woman could be many things besides a wife and a mother. Rebecca decides to place symbols at the statue's feet such as "needle, pen, palette and the ballot-box to show she has earned the right to use them." In the first feminist movement in the early 1900s, women acted behind the scenes. They never directly challenged the authority of men, but rather solicitously encouraged men to "do the right thing."

The women's liberation movement surfaced again in the 1960s when women discovered their voice and stood up for their convictions. Consciousness-raising groups were organized to discuss the negative effects of sexism. In these sessions, women discussed such timely issues as abortion, unequal pay, and the Equal Rights Amendment to the Constitution, which proposed equal rights regardless of gender.

Courage in your convictions creates a sense of honor. Trusting yourself to honor commitments and to stand your ground creates positive energy and contributes pride and dignity to your character. This positive energy gives you the strength to stand up for yourself even though you may face disapproval. Goldie's story reveals these tenets.

| **Goldie: Living Convictions** |

A Woman of Independent Mind

Goldie was one of the earliest feminists. When I interviewed her she had just had a stroke. At age eight-seven, petite, with big blue eyes, she was still driving and playing a mean game of duplicate bridge at the country club. I felt her verve, her passion for life. "I'm not going to live in a nursing home," she vowed, "and I'm not going to go in a wheelchair on a bus again. I don't want to walk with a cane or walker. I want to drive my car again. I'm going to get well!"

Goldie, born in 1910 to a Jewish family, was the youngest of four daughters. Her parents had hoped for a boy. But Goldie became the leader among her sisters, and at twelve years old she learned to drive one of the first Model T Fords, a flivver, while sitting on her dad's lap. Her vision, purpose, stamina, and determination exceeded her sisters' to the very end of her life. While she never looked her age, Goldie knew that personal power lay in thoughts and attitudes, and she never backed down from her values. "Without courage," she insists, "I could not have accomplished what I did."

. . . personal power lay in thoughts and attitudes . . .

One of the first women in her generation to obtain a college degree in educational psychology, she graduated in 1929 at the age of nineteen. Vying for respect, she became one of the first feminists and a founding entrepreneurial businesswomen in her state.

Goldie's father, who owned a salvage company, taught her the "rough and tough" business of liquidating distressed merchandise. She described the trade as "finding a home for things that people would either waste, damage, or throw away." Many times the items were bought unseen from railroad cars. Her father would then reconstruct the goods for another market.

Learning the business came easy for Goldie. She was eager to learn how things worked. What gave her trouble were the men. They would proposition her, coerce her to give them a kickback, or come into the store and demand goods in exchange for their business. She had the courage to stand up to any man. Gradually she gained the respect of her male peers as she held her ground in a very rugged business. By earning this respect, she was able to develop and expand the business later in life.

As Goldie became enamored with the business, she started receiving contracts from stores. "Once I got a call from an agent with a whole load of falsies that came from a swimsuit company," she says proudly. "They were on their way to California when they fell off the truck and got dirty. I took them home, washed them, and wrung hundreds of them through a wringer. I laid them on my Ping-Pong table to dry, then I paired them up and sold them to a manufacturer." Competitive with men at auctions, she eventually came to be trusted for her expertise and knowledge. "I had the courage to research the products we were buying and to become knowledgeable about them."

A widow for many years, Goldie felt she was born with courage and used the phrase "the courage of your convictions." "This is the ability to go through situations following your own inclinations, not always depending on other people's opinions." Goldie's courage supported her struggle to succeed.

The second time I interviewed Goldie she had been ill again. "My life now is rather uneventful," she told me. "I go to an occasional dinner or luncheon. I still drive and belong to a country club where I enjoy playing bridge. Courage may not be as important to me now—I don't think the drive is there like it used to be—but I do know that if something needs to be done, I'll get it done." Goldie felt strongly that women should be able to settle issues in their life using their own power and not be dependent on anyone. My interviews with her were her eulogy and she knew it.

Goldie's final act of courage lay in the dignity with which she lived the last year of her life, enjoying, along with the material things, the personal pride she had worked so hard to achieve. Signing a release form giving me permission to use her story, she wrote: "I am very proud that you have selected me and my life story to be in your book." She died courageously at the age of eighty-eight.

Finding a place where a woman can promote and fulfill her purpose is not easy at any age or in any generation. After Goldie's death, I had a telephone conversation with her son Leslie. He shared with me that he would deliver holiday gifts of bourbon and whiskey to his mother's clients and potential clients. Goldie knew the alcohol would give her an advantage in securing a contract with a railroad or truck line. Leslie recalls, "When I was about sixteen, I realized my mother had a burning desire to succeed. The agents were always nice to me, but I could tell my mother was held to a higher standard. She always had to be up on her game."

Being respected as bright and knowledgeable was always important to Goldie. She took pride in her ability to learn and never abandoned her passion to be a woman of independent mind.

HOW GOLDIE TAPS INTO HER RESERVOIR OF COURAGE TO LIVE HER CONVICTIONS:

- Always be curious. Curiosity is the driving force to accomplishment.
- Be motivated to succeed so you have choices.
- Keep learning.
- Take pride in being dependable and reliable.
- Be known as a troubleshooter in your vocation.
- Understand the customs and behaviors of different people.
- Speak out even when others don't like it.

Goldie's courage gave her purpose and a goal. She never stood still. She independently made the money she needed to do whatever she wanted in her final years. "I always directed my life according to my convictions. I had pride in my reputation and good name."

Manifesting Vision

The bravest thing you can do when you are not brave is profess courage and act accordingly.

Corra May White Harris

BLINDNESS IS NOT A VIRTUE

Vision is how you see yourself and your choices in life. Is your life filled with courage and choices, or is it one mired in a repetition of mistakes? Self-deception can be a problem when you try to create your vision. Blindness is not a virtue! Yet your vision must be designed by your heart, not your eyes. Carl Jung said, "Your vision will become clear only when you look into your heart. Who looks outside dreams; who looks inside, awakens." The right vision—the appropriate, conscious, courageous decisions you make when manifesting your vision—can change your life. Vision leads to greatness.

"Your vision will become clear only when you look into your heart. Who looks outside dreams; who looks inside, awakens."

Dulled by the usual events of your life, you may forget to infuse the gift of courage. You may forget to create a vision. You may forget to question where your self-image comes from. Remember that the strengths that compose the self are instilled and cultivated one by one. Begin to imagine your steps to a life filled with courage. The willingness to create a vision is a statement of your belief in your potential, a bold and courageous declaration that you are in charge.

WHY A NEW VISION?

Developing a new vision frees you from the limitations of the past and opens you up to fresh possibilities. Simply by imagining yourself in new situations, you open your mind to eliminating complacency and routine. You can create a new life. If you call upon your courage to visualize, you can design a life filled with happiness. Carolyn Myss states in *Anatomy of the Spirit*, "View a successful life as a process of achieving self-control and the capacity to work through the challenges life brings you. Visualize success as an energy force rather than a physical one." What you envision holds enormous power. If you can imagine it, you can achieve it!

Kay: Manifesting Vision

Refocusing Goals

Being a high-achiever has taken its toll on Kay's physical well-being and has hampered her vision. I first met Kay when I interviewed her for the book. We found we had a common interest in women's issues. Kay was completing her master's degree in psychology and investigating the impact of stereotypes on women's career advancement. I was surprised to learn she suffered from a severe physical disorder called repetitive stress injury (RSI). She looked fit and healthy; yet, she could no longer use her arm to type and she had to speak into a computer to write.

Kay's physical problem occurred while she was studying for her master's degree and working as a research assistant. She earned $500 a month, worked all day, and would stay up late at night studying and typing. Being a single mother with a five-year-old daughter, she had to borrow money to make ends meet. She was determined to achieve her vision of earning her degree. Nothing was going to stop her, not even harm to her body.

Kay decided to use the courage she felt she was born with to face this problem. She knew how to summon this virtue. When Kay was still in diapers, she wanted to dance like her sisters. She figured there was no reason why she could not join them. As a young girl, she would watch her older sisters do something and then decide she could do it. Her father thought she was just stubborn. Kay says, "Even as a toddler I didn't like being told what I could do. I didn't like the feeling that I was being placed in a box. Limitations were not acceptable. I could see things, both with my eyes and in my mind. That was all it took. I knew I could do it." If she wanted something, Kay went for it. Her family tells her she learned to dance before she learned to walk.

As an adult, Kay was determined to earn her master's degree. She had this vision for a long time and nothing was going to stop her. In her thirties, a single mom close to poverty, Kay sat at her computer every day doing research for her degree. One day, her arm went numb. After lengthy tests, doctors ruled out carpal tunnel syndrome. They discovered the numbness in her arm was related to her neck. Her condition was called thoracic outlet syndrome.

For Kay, this adult disability triggered the same childhood response she'd had when she wanted to dance. "I resisted someone trying to limit me. I wanted to say to the doctors: I am different. I am going to dance, not walk." If someone told her she could not do something, she wanted to prove them wrong. All she had to do was visualize her goal and her courage gave her the strength to accomplish it.

This stubborn streak, along with Kay's ability to turn a vision into a concrete plan, helped her face her disability. Her energetic approach propelled her to overcome this setback. However, raising her daughter made her disability even more frustrating. "There were times when my daughter wanted me to comb her hair or help her learn to ride her bicycle, but the pain in my arm prevented my helping her."

In these situations, Kay was unable to pursue her vision. "It was terrible," she says, "I felt like I was letting my daughter down."

Kay thinks her stubbornness may have been why she chose to study stereotypes. Being placed in a stereotypical box was never an option for her. She was determined to persevere even at the risk of physical health. She discovered an article called "Women Working in the Margin" by Virginia Shine, who has researched women in poverty. Shine found that single, poverty-stricken mothers who work and go to school often have RSI. Kay saw herself in the research. She mused, "Here I was, using my courage to override these same setbacks."

Finishing her master's degree at age thirty-six, Kay put her Ph.D. vision on hold. It hurt to breathe, to stand, and to read. She went to a physical therapist and a physical trainer. While the pain will always be there, it has subsided to some degree. "I am still not sure if I can go on to get my Ph.D. It would be so stressful and taxing to my body. The tasks would require me to hold a book up to read for long hours. I still want to, but the time is not right. It is difficult for me to give myself permission to wait so long." Kay's drive to succeed is unmatched in most women with a disability.

One of the hardest shifts for Kay was mustering the courage to admit to other people that she had a disability. She confessed, "I don't let people see me using my voice-activated computer, although I did allow my computer adaptive-technology guy to interview me and to take pictures for a presentation at a disability conference." Kay agreed to it because she felt it would help other people achieve their goals.

Courage is an integral part of Kay's life. Sometimes it takes courage to stop when the physical pain starts. Other times it takes courage to take better care of herself, such as going to physical therapy. The courage to ask for help and reveal vulnerability is also coming easier. She says it still takes a lot of courage for her to not get depressed when her plans for the future are slowed by the reality of her disability. Even though the vision of her timetable has changed, she vows, "I'm going to make it. I'm still going to perform. I'm still going to get my work done—just maybe a little differently." When she would start to feel *dis*couraged, Kay visualizes her body with no pain, calls on her courage, and envisions a plan.

"Truly courageous people have a vision, a mission," Kay continues. "It's a piece of who you are." Regardless of the outcome, her vision drives her to achieve her dreams. "I think in order to be successful, courage must come from the heart. It is a guiding voice that keeps me on my course."

"Truly courageous people have a vision, a mission. . . . It's a piece of who you are."

Almost a year after our interview, I called Kay to inquire about her health. She is enjoying a new career and will be remarrying next year. With the chronic pain almost gone, she feels the roller-coaster ride is over. "I'm beginning to climb the mountain again. I can see the possibility of the journey. I can see the top again."

How Kay Taps into Her Reservoir of Courage to Manifest a Vision:

- Develop a "stubborn streak."
- Resist labels placed on you by others.
- Discard judgments.
- Ask yourself: How will I use my courage to tackle this situation?

- Let go of pride.
- Keep learning.
- Use courage as a choice to go forward.
- Do not avoid the situation.
- Walk through pain in order to get well.
- Grow. Acquire courage with every step of your vision.

Kay is proud of her courage and recognizes its value. Courage is her friend. It remains a favorite tool while she strives for her vision. She envisions a blanket of courage wrapped around her, a blanket that protects her as she faces the unknown.

"Courage becomes familiar, like holding the hand of a loving companion."

"Courageous behavior occurs more often once you decide you're going to be a courageous woman. Courage becomes familiar, like holding the hand of a loving companion."

Overcoming Illness or Loss

Don't be afraid your life will end;
be afraid that it will never begin.

Grace Hansen

MAINTAINING BALANCE

As our culture struggles with redefining roles for men and women, the unspoken expectations of femininity become part of a woman's personality. These subtle messages often diminish her sense of self-worth and cripple her ability to live a purposeful life. Another dimension of personal courage requires rejecting externally imposed definitions of what it means to be a woman in a particular time and place.

Another dimension of personal courage requires rejecting externally imposed definitions of what it means to be a woman . . .

Too often our culture defines women by their physical appearance, causing women to identify primarily with their bodies rather than with their minds or spirits. Such undue attention to physical appearance can go to absurd lengths. Anorexia and bulimia have become epidemic in this country. It is not surprising that girls as young as eleven can suffer from eating disorders, which usually begin during adolescence or early adulthood. Ninety percent of anorexia nervosa (an ancient illness) sufferers are women. This chronic and even fatal illness afflicts approximately 77,000 people in the United States.

It takes courage to reject the destructive messages that our culture perpetuates about a woman's appearance and to overcome the self-destructive behaviors such messages can foster. Women are made to feel they need to be perfect in so many ways—the perfect lover, the perfect wife, the perfect mother, and the perfect career professional. And they need to do it all wearing a perfect size-six dress.

Self-infliction has been around for a long time. Spiritual saints, including St. Catherine of Siena, sought to be closer to God by imitating Christ's suffering on the cross. At six years of age, in 1353, after St. Catherine experienced her first vision of Christ, she and her friends began to flagellate themselves in secret and tormented themselves with extreme fasting in order to prove their obedience to God. Several years later, she tried to reverse her acute

126

fasting, but it was too late. Her frail body would no longer tolerate food. At the end of her life she urged other women not to follow her example. She died of starvation at the age of thirty-three. Unfortunately, many Italian girls did not heed her warning; they starved themselves to emulate her, just as young women today starve themselves to emulate their favorite fashion models, movie stars, or television personalities.

Diana, Princess of Wales, spoke openly of her bulimia, providing a major breakthrough in recognition of the disease. She was a charismatic example of a woman whose visible pain inspired passionate devotion. Some thought her a modern-day saint who suffered self-inflicted torments while trying to help others.

In the article, "Power Suffering," Jennifer Egan stated, "Even as our culture decries these disorders, in subtle ways it endorses the equation of suffering with female power; what was heroin chic if not a study of the stark beauty of feminine duress, a beauty that seemed to pulse forth with even greater intensity from the scrawny, bruised-looking models with raccoon eyes and hair tangled to perfection."

Only when women have the courage to set aside the masks that fad and fashion dictate . . .

Such distorted notions of beauty are madness. Only when women have the courage to set aside the masks that fad and fashion dictate will they discover that they are loved for who they are, not how well they conform to impossible, often destructive images. Only then will they find inner peace.

Candace: Overcoming Illness

Reflection in the Mirror

For Candace, a married forty-one-year-old college graduate with one son, it took physical courage to get through her four-year addiction to bulimia. She shared with me that when she read transcripts of her interviews it brought back all of the feelings of despair and pain. At one point, she didn't want to go forward with the interviews because she was embarrassed and ashamed that she had hurt herself in that way.

It took Candace almost two years to want to stop throwing up everything she ate. She says, "For many years I didn't face the harm of bulimia because I was so busy thinking about how to be a successful bulimic. I was focused on hiding my behavior, not changing it. I spent countless hours fooling myself into thinking it had to be an illness rather than a decision." One time after her routine vomiting, she saw blood in the toilet bowl and she knew she was throwing up her stomach lining, throwing away her health. Frightened, she realized she was ruining her body. Not only the physical damage, but the emotional pain, of trying to maintain an unrealistic weight was killing her. She had to stop.

Candace finally recognized that bulimia was a choice. She also knew that if she stopped she would probably lose her boyfriend, a man who valued her thinness over all else. But she had to face the reality of continuing to be bulimic. The reality was illness and death.

Candace discovered and studied the book *The Course in Miracles.* Its purpose is to alter one's de-structive perceptions. During her study she came to believe that God would help her with her recovery. She felt that she would eventually find peace by working through the course. She believed that if she changed her thinking, she could change her behavior. She would not be a victim of an illness; she was a person with the power to choose her actions. Courage is a state of being.

Day after difficult day, Candace faced the illness until it was not tempting anymore. If she thought she ate too much, she could choose to throw up or she could manage her eating for the rest of the day. Candace credits *The Course in Miracles* and the unconditional support from her mother and sister with her recovery from bulimia. "I realized I must take responsibility to consciously eat too much or too little," Candace said. "It just didn't make sense to harm myself when I could choose otherwise." She felt the most powerful statement in the course was: "Teach only love, for that is what you are."

Courage is a state of being.

Candace found the affirmations in *The Course in Miracles* very powerful. They helped her resist bulimic temptation and were pivotal to her recovery.

> *The past is over. I can see peace instead of this.*
> *God's voice speaks to me all through the day.*

Candace now understands that perfectionism is impossible. Being thin is no longer a competitive issue. "The most courageous step in this whole process is that I value myself no matter what the package looks like."

How Candace Taps into Her Reservoir of Courage to Overcome Illness:

- Say affirmations from *The Course in Miracles*.
- Face experiences rather than running from them.

- Marry someone who values you for you, not for thinness.
- Accept who you are. Strive for accomplishment, not perfection.
- Have a vision and focus.
- Seek a healthy role model.
- Surround yourself with people who will support you.
- Realize you have the power of choice.

"Using my courage, I could face one morning at a time, one afternoon at a time, and one evening at a time, without going crazy."

For Candace, courage is not just a way of thinking; being courageous means taking action. Courage gave her the ability to recover from a devastating disease and to emerge stronger and whole. "Using my courage, I could face one morning at a time, one afternoon at a time, and one evening at a time, without going crazy. I use this approach to handle all challenges in my life."

Facing Loss

Those who don't know how to weep with their whole heart don't know how to laugh either.

Golda Meir

Every woman utilizes three kinds of courage. The first kind requires only a little fortitude, such as giving blood or speaking up at a PTA meeting. The second requires more bravery, such as revealing a long-held secret. The third kind is spiritual courage, the courage needed to recover from the loss of something or someone we hold dear. Spiritual courage is powerful indeed and requires all of our strength and hope. But with it comes an inner knowledge that we are safe in infinite love.

> ## Diane: Facing Loss

Releasing Love

Broken hearts mend slowly. Diane, who speaks in a soft and self-assured manner, has been through a lot in her forty-one years. She feels courage has been her guiding force throughout.

Broken hearts mend slowly.

Diane stayed in an abusive cycle for years, leaving her husband six times. Most of the time her husband put her down with verbal abuse and name-calling. He would call her a whore and accuse her of being unfaithful. At one point Diane's husband called her boss's wife and told her that Diane was having an affair with her husband.

Diane returned to her husband after each abusive incident because he would apologize, buy her flowers, and say he loved her. She hoped his words meant he would change. Diane had been conditioned to accept this kind of abuse. Her father had disciplined his children physically, and had hit Diane many times for trivial offenses such as not folding a dishcloth correctly. Her father also verbally abused Diane, making her feel that she was never good enough.

Diane worried constantly about her sons, feeling it was only a matter of time before her husband would start abusing them. Summoning her courage, she finally escaped from her husband and moved across the country with her children. Living in a shelter for battered women, she found comfort in sharing her story of abuse. She could not remember the last time she had smiled.

After learning from the shelter's supervisor that her husband had threatened her boss and secretary to tell him where she was hiding, and faced with reinventing her life in a new city, Diane changed her name and her sons' names. As an additional precaution, she changed their Social Security numbers and broke contact with her parents and friends. Only her brother and sister-in-law knew her plan and provided encouragement. Diane said, "I could not have done this drastic life change without their support because I felt scared and wanted to give up many times throughout my journey."

Diane's definition of courage is the ability to identify internal weaknesses and to change them into strengths. Six months after acquiring her new identity, she met Steve in a ballroom-dance class. They took every dance lesson they could so they could be together. From country to swing, they fell in love trying to keep step to the beat. He treated her and her children wonderfully. They camped and fished and traveled throughout Diane's newly adopted state. She reflects, "You could just see the goodness in Steve. His love was unconditional."

Diane knew when she married Steve that he had been diagnosed with a very rare type of cancer called nasalpharyngeal. But this life-threatening illness did not dissuade Steve from wanting to provide for Diane and the boys. Though at first they felt optimistic about their future, it soon became apparent that Steve did not have long to live. After enduring a twenty-two hour surgery, he stayed in the hospital for weeks.

During the Christmas season, Steve, only fifty-one, told her he was ready to give up and disconnected his feeding tube. Grief stricken, Diane knew she had to let go of the only man she had ever loved, the only one who had truly loved her. The two of them reminisced about all they had done together. "We openly expressed our love for each other. I said all the things I wanted to say and he said what he wanted to say. Sometimes I would crawl in bed with him and hold him."

Diane wanted to keep Steve alive as long as possible. But she knew Steve was ready to let go of his suffering. She knew he found comfort knowing that she was not going to stop him from removing the feeding tube. She loved him enough to allow him to die. This took tremendous courage. She cherished the love she had, and knew she would eventually get through her loss. Diane was with Steve as he took his last breath.

Diane concluded, "We all stumble, we all have weaknesses, and we all have strengths. Different qualities within us drive each one of us, so I'm not much different from any other woman. I still have so much I want to do, and that will move me on."

"We all stumble, we all have weaknesses, and we all have strengths."

HOW DIANE TAPS INTO HER RESERVOIR OF COURAGE TO FACE LOSS:

- Ask for help. Isolation is the opposite of courage.
- Seek other people.
- Maintain open communication with your children.
- Be aware of your anger.
- Distinguish surviving and courage.
- Believe you have a choice.
- Create a vision of where you want to go.
- Use resiliency to push courage to the surface.

• Say affirmations, such as "I can do it!"

Diane trusts her instincts after all she has been through. When people tell her she is courageous, she believes them. She knows she is worthy and that she deserves to have a good life. She remains true to herself by not letting the wishes of others define her identity. "The escape from my abusive situation caused me to leave my cruel husband and to find love again, so I know I can conquer anything. It doesn't matter that I didn't think of myself as courageous as a little girl. I learned to become courageous—it was a hidden quality deep inside my spirit and always there. Finding it has made all the difference."

"I learned to become courageous—it was a hidden quality deep inside my spirit and always there."

Reflecting Self-Esteem

*We don't see things as they are,
we see them as we are.*

Anaïs Nin

FEELING GOOD ABOUT YOURSELF

Problems with self-esteem usually can be traced to patterns established as a child. A child's sense of self is formed through her relationship with her parents, particularly the mother. A person with healthy self-esteem feels good about herself and is able to withstand criticism, rejection, or failure. She maintains a positive self-image. The opinions of others do not immobilize her or cause doubt. When she makes a mistake or fails to achieve a goal, she uses courage to overcome her disappointment.

| **Tracy: Reflecting Self-Esteem** |

Restoring True Self

Thirty-one-year-old Tracy has a college degree in political science. Single and working in the telecommunications industry, she believes courage is an innate trait. Always the tallest in her class and the first to do things, Tracy hung out with boys, played with trucks and Legos, and never liked dolls. She feels courage is synonymous with goodness. "I've never thought of myself as not courageous."

When Tracy arrived for her post-behavioral interview, she looked stressed and tired. She felt bad she had gained some weight and started smoking again. "I'm sorry to say that at this time in my life I'm not full of courage," she said. "Right now I need to dive in and find the courage to reclaim my self-esteem. I know this process requires looking inside myself for the problem and then meditating on the subject." For many of us, the norms of sexual attractiveness are the index of our self-esteem.

It had not been an easy year for Tracy. She switched jobs only to discover that her new boss was unethical. "I've had to fight my boss to uphold my values," she said. "My self-esteem has been torn down during these exchanges. In some ways, the Tracy I know is disappearing. I'm not as vivacious or as positive about things as I usually am."

Tracy's courage had become dormant. She had been ignoring her heart and spirit. Depressed, she

A person with healthy self-esteem feels good about herself and is able to withstand criticism, rejection, or failure.

couldn't visualize what steps she should take to re-claim her happiness. With her self-esteem and courage at a low point, she found it hard to moti-vate herself to look into her soul to reclaim them. "Since I did the initial book interview," she said, "I've thought about the word *courage* more than ever, but right now I'm in a rut. I need to rescue the real Tracy—the Tracy I shared when we first met. It's easy to use my courage when I'm feeling good about myself. Then I'm strong and powerful. But it's much harder when I'm down."

When asked if she thought her courage had dis-appeared, she replied, "I don't think so. I think it's always there. For me, the way to utilize it is to strengthen my self-esteem. I am most courageous when I have a great attitude about myself."

"Courage is nagging at my heels."

Though she believes she was born with courage, she cautioned, "But it can die out. Right now I am fighting to rekindle it. Courage is nagging at my heels."

Almost a year later, I called Tracy to inquire how she was fighting the battle to reclaim her courage. She sounded great and expressed that she was very happy. I asked her how she adjusted her behavior. She shared with me that it took courage to evaluate the situation, that it was not in her best interest to stay in a working environment that destroyed her self-worth. Courage allowed her to leave her job without a future plan in place.

Angry, yet determined, Tracy told herself, "This is tearing me apart. I have to stand up for myself—this situation is not good physically, emotionally, or men-tally for me. I need to leave, even though I don't know where my next paycheck is coming from."

After she left her job, Tracy knew she was going

to be struggling financially for a while. She reasoned, "It was better than leaving myself open for more degradation. I connected concretely with the heart of my courage to rebuild my self-esteem, which fuels my strength, inner power, and beauty." Tracy called this process the "courage effect" because her self-confidence kicked in with each step taken. She explained, "I found that once I regained my self-confidence everything fell into place. I am at the strongest point of my life, even though I may weigh the most I've ever weighed."

Tracy became more vulnerable to people by allowing them to see her weaknesses, such as her habit of pretending to be happy. She said, "I now connect with people more deeply by holding their gaze longer, smiling more, and shaking their hands more firmly. People sense my ability to open myself up to them. I allow them to share in my energy—I am no longer hiding behind my low self-esteem. During my depression I faked my self-confidence. Now that I have rekindled my courage, my self-confidence is completely genuine."

"I connected concretely with the heart of my courage to rebuild my self-esteem, which fuels my strength, inner power, and beauty."

HOW TRACY TAPS INTO HER RESERVOIR OF COURAGE TO REFLECT SELF-ESTEEM:

- Look inside yourself and ask: What do I need to do to change?
- Conduct a self-audit by writing on a piece of paper "I am . . ." sentences.
- Remember who you are and what you stand for.
- Surround yourself with active, outgoing people.
- Sharpen your skills and abilities through education, reading, and training.
- Allow yourself to be vulnerable.

Tracy tackles problems head on. But when she

feels depressed, she has to get back in touch with her true self. "I say to myself that I am a smart girl and I can do it. I can face this funk and dig myself out and become the self-confident person I want to be. I just have to admit that I'm in a funk in order to mobilize."

Reinventing Self

> *It's never too late to be what*
> *you might have been.*

> George Eliot

CHOOSING A NEW LIFE PATTERN

Courage is a force that projects outwardly from the heart, a part of the self. And it can reinvent the self when you have temporarily lost your way. That new self can lead to a whole new life pattern.

Reinventing yourself in order to transcend rejection or other negative experiences requires full employment of your personal courage. When you take a stand, you must be willing to face the possibility that everyone may not agree with you. Think through the likely reactions of others and prepare alternative responses. You do not want to lose your identity when your ideas are rebuffed. You are not required to alter yourself to comply with the beliefs of others. At that moment rely upon your understanding of yourself, your opinions, and your values.

Accept responsibility for the shaping of your innermost self. Call upon your courage to stand up for the self you know to be you.

Princess Diana had no choice but to reinvent herself. Several of the women interviewed for this book felt that Diana personified courage. She faced criticism and controversy no matter where she turned—not just from the press and photographers, but from gossips, speculators, and even her friends. She was cast out and rebuffed by the monarchy. Yet, she mustered the courage to maintain her dignity and compassion for others.

Call upon your courage to stand up for the self you know to be you.

For a long time Princess Diana suffered from bulimia and low self-esteem. Required to pretend her marriage was a happy one, she felt unloved and unsupported. She wanted to reach out to people when they were in their "dark tunnels."

With all her strengths and weaknesses, Diana was a real person to real people. Just like the women in this book. Just like you. She could empathize with others because of her own experiences of distress. After her divorce from Prince Charles, she needed time to reinvent herself. Tragically a fatal car accident ended her quest for a new life.

Most of us do have time to reinvent ourselves. When a woman fails to tackle a challenge she knows she can and should meet, particularly after something—or someone—has robbed her of her identity, it is often because she is crushed by self-doubt. She will question her ability to succeed. Courage is the impetus to reinvent yourself and redirect your course.

Sue: Reinventing Self

Reclaiming Identity

Sue is a human resource manager for a manufacturing company. Fifty-five years old, warm and positive with piercing blue eyes, she defines courage as, "the willingness to take risks and to try new things, like a new career; to keep going when you think it might be easier to give up."

In 1962, in a small midwestern town, Sue had just graduated from high school when she became pregnant by the man she had been dating for more than a year. She was raised with strong values and morals, and though she did not feel prepared for marriage, she married and committed herself to her husband and their daughter.

She had never held a job, except for helping her dad at a bank. However, to help support her new family, she asked the dean of the college her husband was attending if she could work as a secretary. She did all the things women were expected to do to make their husbands successful and to maintain a happy home. "For the first couple of years, we were just two kids raising a child. It took courage for me to stay in a marriage that was far from perfect. I worked hard at it, like a good girl should." Fortunate to have a loving grandmother to care for their daughter, Sue worked at the college for ten years.

Sue believes that she has always had a small amount of courage, though was not aware of it. She feels she was not born with it, but learned to be courageous through the necessity to survive. Being courageous was not a part of her upbringing because her family environment did not promote independent women. Her courage was suppressed during her marriage; she was not courageous because she was dependent on her husband.

After thirty years of marriage, her world fell apart. Her husband told her he didn't want to be married to her anymore. "I couldn't imagine my life without him. I had never lived on my own. I had gone directly from my parents' home into marriage. It was even scary for me to be alone in our big house."

. . . she was not courageous because she was dependent on her husband.

Sue did not want to grow old feeling bitter about her divorce. Yet it was a difficult time for her. "It took a lot of courage to go to work every day. During breaks I would go into the bathroom and cry. Sometimes I would cry all the way home and when I got home, I'd cry some more." She began seeing a counselor at her church and a psychotherapist. Both were a great help to her during that painful transition.

Today, Sue's career challenges her to use the resources she discovered in coping with her divorce. "I put myself at risk to totally reinvent myself, and my self-esteem allowed me to keep my boundaries. Now I can say no to what I don't want or need. Learning to say no was especially difficult. But I now know I can do whatever I want in my life. The whole process has made me better at my job. I became a human resources manager, and a lot of the people who come to me are experiencing the same kinds of problems that I went through. I'm not sure I could have empathized with people the way I can now if I hadn't experienced the heartache and turmoil of my divorce." Sue lost her identity as a wife but reinvented herself as an independent professional.

In the year that has passed since her first interview, Sue has taken a new position at a high-tech company, earning a promotion to director of Human Resources after three months. She has also fallen in love with a man for the first time since her divorce five years ago. She says, "I can certainly see how having the courage to reinvent myself played a critical role in getting what I wanted in my life." She admits that she uses the word *courage* now more than ever when she coaches employees.

Visualizing a situation, and playing it out in your mind, supports your change in behavior by preparing you for potential rejection.

Sue recognizes that others have the right to their own opinions, and this insight allows her not to take rejection personally. She avoids magnifying perceived rejection, which might leave her with negative feelings about herself. Sue is living proof of a fulfilled life.

Creating a strategy to cope with rejection is helpful. Visualizing a situation, and playing it out in your mind, supports your change in behavior by preparing you for potential rejection. It allows you to "save face" (maintain integrity) by being prepared. Imagining (and role-playing) the worst possible scenario defuses the real situation.

We are all products of our past experiences. But dwelling on these past events is not healing. Such nonconstructive behavior only mires us deeper into our rut; we remain entrenched in our wounds. Caroline Myss, Ph.D., writes; "They [wounded people] have redefined their lives around their wounds and the process of accepting them. They are not working to get beyond those wounds." Moving beyond the wounds of incest, abuse, abandonment, or rejection allows us to get on with the business of living a happy and fulfilled life.

Repositioning takes courage, and integrating

courage moves us to make different choices. Many times we have to experience a crisis before we can move forward because we are not committed to movement. We become stuck in one place, wearing different faces with the same name. Sue's divorce crisis motivated her to move ahead. She coped with rejection and reinvented herself to live a fulfilled life. "Because of what I've gone through and the transitions I've made, I feel I'm a totally different woman who now sees a new and exciting challenge in what I once would have thought impossible."

HOW SUE TAPS INTO HER RESERVOIR OF COURAGE TO REINVENT HERSELF:

- Nurture strong beliefs and values.
- Choose to move forward.
- Develop good friendships.
- Be independent.
- Have faith.
- Stand by your beliefs.
- Never be a quitter, always be a winner.
- Study the situation. Make wise choices.
- Take risks.

Sue believes that once you recognize you have courage, you gain strength. After her divorce, she began to look at herself differently. She now sees herself as strong and confident. She believes we all have courage; we just need to recognize the courage stored inside each of us. "For me, the predominant source of my courage is my faith. I do not take courage lightly. I chose not to be a bitter woman. Courage helps me succeed by reinventing who I am in a positive way."

"Courage helps me succeed by reinventing who I am in a positive way."

Revealing Vulnerability

*It's better to be a lion for a day
than a sheep all your life.*

Sister Elizabeth Kenny

TRUST ENOUGH TO REVEAL YOUR HEART

Establishing an emotional connection with people
requires exposing vulnerabilities. You may fear that
if you open up to someone, and show your true
feelings to reveal who you really are, you might get
hurt. Yet, you cannot know real intimacy unless you
are willing to make yourself emotionally vulnerable
to someone else.

Many people in our culture do not let down their
emotional defenses because they do not trust anyone enough to do so. As a result, they build even
higher emotional walls around themselves, keeping
their feelings isolated and blocked from exposure.
Having the courage to communicate feelings dis-
solves those emotional barriers and brings you
closer to people. The key to interpersonal relationships is having the courage to be open and vulnerable. Once you reveal a carefully guarded secret
about yourself, you will find that the repressed fear
and inhibition associated with the secret loses its
power.

Mary Catherine Bateson writes, in *Composing a Life*,
"There are two kinds of vulnerabilities that women
raised in our society tend to have. The first is the quality of self-sacrifice, a learned willingness to set their

*. . . you
cannot know
real intimacy
unless you are
willing to
make yourself
emotionally
vulnerable to
someone else.*

own interest aside and be used and even used up by their community. The second kind of vulnerability trained into women is a readiness to believe messages of disdain and derogation—distorted visions of them-selves—no longer secure that their sense of who they are matches the perceptions of others."

Yet admitting you feel these and other vulnerabil-ities can rid you of them. It's like releasing a caged bird and watching it soar. That which we fear to ac-knowledge holds us in its bondage, but, once rec-ognized, it loses its control over us.

> *That which we fear to acknowledge holds us in its bondage, but, once recognized, it loses its control over us.*

Carol: Revealing Vulnerability

Rendezvous with Unfinished Business

Carol believed that vulnerability represents weakness. She felt that she must keep her guard up and not ex-pose her true feelings. When she was thirty-six years old and happily married to her second husband, her world was turned upside down. After undergoing a partial hysterectomy, she became clinically depressed. She battled the dark times for seven years, began see-ing a Jungian psychiatrist to treat her chemical unbal-ance and help her face her painful past.

Physically and sexually abused when she was a child, Carol reveals, "There was a crew member on my father's flight team who took advantage of me as a little girl. My father also sexually abused me. When I would go out for a run, I had flashbacks of the abuse. I struggled with serious depression and feelings of loneliness."

But Carol did not want to be committed to a men-tal institution. She chose to fight through the isola-tion her illness had produced. Working with a psychiatrist who told her that human beings go into

145

depression for a reason, her illness became a time of reflection.

In Chapter Two, Carol shared how much she loved the movie the *The Wizard of Oz*. She remembers that she used to go around the house imitating the Lion. Now, at forty-eight, she has learned to be courageous even when it requires being vulnerable. "I still struggle with showing vulnerability. I still have a hard time crying, probably because when my father would hit me he wanted me to cry and I wouldn't. That's my stubbornness."

Recently, Carol talked with a co-worker who was dealing with an abusive husband. Carol, who had been in an abusive relationship with her first husband, was able to give the woman some advice. She told her, "You need to actively change the situation. Get help and develop strength. You can't allow the situation to go on. You must be courageous to get out of the marriage."

HOW CAROL TAPS INTO HER RESERVOIR OF COURAGE TO REVEAL VULNERABILITY:

- Assess your current situation and start making plans for change.
- Stand up for yourself by speaking up.
- Be aware of your feelings and use them to change the situation.
- Observe your patterns of thinking.
- Pray for guidance.
- Listen to the little voice inside.
- Trust your gut feelings.
- Be vulnerable by expressing your feelings.
- Merge being stubborn with courage.

For Carol, courage is a strong internal force. It allows her to say what she needs to say and to make the situation right. Her motivation comes from her heart and it gives her the power to do what needs to be done. She knows that courage is genderless. She approaches problems with confidence. Carol often prays: "God, you know what happened to me in the past. I got through all of that and I'm able to be where I am now. I'm so blessed." Having learned the value of being vulnerable, she concludes, "I try to respond with vulnerability from my heart. I expose more of me and let more people in."

"I try to respond with vulnerability from my heart. I expose more of me and let more people in."

Speaking Up

Ask the Light to enter the fear and give you the courage not to act in that negative pattern again.

Caroline Myss, Ph.D.
Anatomy of the Spirit

MAKING YOUR VOICE HEARD

Courage involves speaking up for what is right and good. Courage is maintaining your own voice and not standing passively by when you witness injustice. Such courage is inside every woman. When you summon courage from the depths of your heart and spirit, you will find your voice.

The courage to speak up is more than just being assertive. Being assertive means behaving in a direct way to achieve your goals. Speaking up is an essential part of self-respect. The courage to speak up also means that you put yourself first. Keeping quiet about your ideas, feelings, and desires because you fear disapproval puts you in an inferior position. Speaking up allows you to live according to your values.

The courage to speak up provides a woman with authenticity.

The courage to speak up provides a woman with authenticity. Censoring yourself fosters powerlessness. Saying what you think, even at the risk of disagreeing with others, gives you further strength. Trusting your voice allows you to retain your integrity. Don't censor yourself. Asking for what you want and standing up for your convictions—validating your womanhood—will benefit not only you but your family and friends, your employer, and your community.

Ruthie: Speaking Up

Nurturing Your Inclinations

Ruthie, now twenty-eight and married with no children, was always on the fast educational track. In junior high, she was tested for placement in the advanced science and mathematics programs. She scored the same as a boy in her class and became extremely upset when the boy was accepted into the advanced classes and she was not. With support of her parents, she talked to the principal. She recalled, "I was really going against the authority, but I took a stand to speak up and fought the decision. In the end I still wasn't accepted, but I did speak up against the injustice. That's the important thing. And I was pleased when a friend pointed out my courage."

Today, Ruthie promotes the economic development of a major international airport. She feels that everyone at some level possesses at least small levels of courage. "Courage shows up in every part of our lives. The derivation of courage, *cor*, means the heart. I think that's true—it comes from the heart. It's the willingness to step over the precipice. Even if you fall into that precipice, you pull yourself out, you brush yourself off, and keep moving. Girls are taught that risk is bad, that failure is bad. The willingness to fail is an act of courage."

"The willingness to fail is an act of courage."

HOW RUTHIE TAPS INTO HER RESERVOIR OF COURAGE TO SPEAK UP:

- Do a self-evaluation. Look at your situation and determine how your courage can overcome or move beyond the circumstance. Find the issue that is keeping you from moving forward.
- Identify what you have control over and what you don't have control over. Can you influence the issue or not? Remain flexible.
- Communicate your fear to someone. Say it out loud.
- Surround yourself with positive influences. Attitudes of those around you—parents or friends—are important to your courage.
- Do what you feel is the right thing—for you.
- Take on new responsibilities at work. When procrastination or a disinclination to take action sets in, tackle small additional tasks. Successes will give you confidence to move ahead.
- Face the unknown and move outside your comfort zone.

"Courage is a basic human virtue. It needs to be encouraged."

Ruthie still has the courage to step out in front of a situation when she does not necessarily know how it is going to be resolved. She does not like to fail. Courage for her is a resource that lies in her flexibility. "Courage is a basic human virtue. It needs to be *en*couraged. It takes courage on my

149

part to step back and let people find their own paths. Life throws unexpected twists. It's then that the ability to act courageously can make the difference between restoring and maintaining a satisfying life or sinking into despair."

Sarah: Speaking Up

Giving Voice to Your Principles

Sarah is another young woman who speaks up for what she believes to be right. When she was in high school, a male teacher wanted to hold a closed-door conference with Sarah after she had misbehaved in class. His simple request triggered a dreadful memory: a high school teacher had raped her older sister when Sarah was twelve. A voice inside warned her that the teacher's insistence on a closed-door meeting was inappropriate.

Sarah chose to stand up to her teacher. She paid a steep price. The teacher kicked her out of the class for refusing to meet with him behind closed doors. Looking back, Sarah has no regrets about what she did in that awkward situation. She has since discovered that when someone attempts to suppress her courage and she says nothing, she risks losing something very precious—a key part of her spirit. She says, "I adamantly believe that courage means voicing your position in all situations, whether personal or work-related. Don't ever give away your voice or allow yourself to be silenced!"

"Don't ever give away your voice or allow yourself to be silenced!"

It is not surprising that Sarah, twenty-six years old with a degree in journalism and sociology, feels courage is a state of mind that shows in every part of our lives. She says, "Courage is the ability to move forward. It's just a daily thing that enables you to do new and different things that may be uncomfortable or fearful."

How Sarah Taps into Her Reservoir of Courage to Speak Up

- Listen to the voice inside of you.
- Set your boundaries.
- Exercise your courageous voice daily. Don't let it be stripped away.
- Know the voice of your courage.
- Believe your intuition and notice if you are uncomfortable.
- Tell people why you are uncomfortable with a situation.
- Challenge the status quo.
- Make waves when someone is putting you down.

Sarah is surprised that women of Generation X (the "Busters" born between 1966–1981) do not extend themselves more with their voices. She said, "Men are taught to stretch themselves. If I have a daughter, I want her to know she is beautiful and smart, that she can do whatever she wants. I don't want her to be in a relationship where a man or woman silences her. I want my little girl to be proud to be a girl."

Sarah concluded, "The more you use your voice, the more courageous you become. It's not about screaming out bold statements. You just want people around you to know that you have a voice. They know you are courageous, so they challenge you less—there are boundaries. They respect your standards."

Is Courage a Part of Your Behavior?

As you ponder the Behaviors of Courage exhibited by these stories, consider those that are already part of your personality—and those that you hope to incorporate into a vision for your life. Keep in mind, true moral courage comes from doing what you believe is right. When necessary, call upon your courage for the strength to stand up for yourself. A healthy self-image comes not from going along with the majority, not from seeking refuge in conventional patterns or ideas, but from being true to yourself and to your vision.

A strong self-image that radiates courage mobilizes your feminine energy.

Fear of rejection or disapproval is a strong inhibition to change. It takes courage to take a stand. It takes courage to speak up when a cold shoulder is turned to you. It takes courage to stop injustice by confronting it openly. It takes courage to let go of denial and face the truth about an illness or loss. It takes courage to have faith when hope seems gone, and to remain strong and determined in the face of setbacks. It takes courage to acknowledge fears and vulnerabilities, and to admit to being afraid.

Focus on your vision for a satisfying life. Your image of yourself is the single most telling factor in determining your ultimate success and happiness. A strong self-image that radiates courage mobilizes your feminine energy. When you act from the heart you fill your reservoir of courage to the brim. Dare to risk. Your courage will see you through.

PART FOUR

ACTION

ACTION

ACTION FROM YOUR HEART

Courage is the force that shapes your life. It is an innate part of womankind although social mores, belief systems, and traditions may have distorted it. A woman's reservoir of courage is a self-renewing resource. It propels you to transform yourself. Tapping into your potential to find courage is like finding unlimited compassion, hope, wisdom, and confidence. As your potential to include courage increases, internal changes occur, your character is strengthened, and more control is established to take on each hurdle in your life.

A woman's reservoir of courage is a self-renewing resource.

Courageous action can be verbal, as well as physical. Language, too, is a powerful force that shapes your life. So if you reinvent yourself, reinforce your courage, and transform your potential, simply being attentive to language can help you jump-start your resolve.

If you identify and appreciate instances of courage in your life, you will honor yourself as courageous. If you recognize the link between language and action, you will create a whole new universe of possibilities for yourself.

Courage can be the fuel of hope that animates and enriches your life's journey. Language is the seasoning that enhances your courageous choices.

CONSCIOUS CHOICE

+

LANGUAGE

+

ACTION FROM THE HEART

=

COURAGE

CHAPTER NINE

THE LANGUAGE OF COURAGE

Words are a form of action,
capable of influencing change.

Ingrid Bengis

CHANGE YOUR WORDS, CHANGE YOUR LIFE

Sticks and stones may break my bones, but words can never hurt me. This old adage is false. Words can hurt you. The language you use and live by can perpetuate the behavior you are trying to dismantle.

"It is through language that we create the world, because it's nothing until we describe it. And when we describe it, we create distinctions that govern our actions. To put it another way, "we do not describe the world we see, but we see the world we describe." Thus wrote Joseph Jaworski in *Synchronicity: The Inner Path of Leadership,* in which he comments on his discussions with biologist Francisco Varela, a professor of cognitive science and coauthor of *The Tree of Knowledge.*

"Our language and our nervous system combine to constantly construct our environment," Jaworski says. "We can only see what we talk about, because we are speaking 'blind'—beyond language. Language provides another set of eyes and hands for the nervous system, through which we coordi-

". . . we do not describe the world we see, but we see the world we describe."

157

nate our actions with others. We exist in language. We exist in a world of distinctions."

Language provides the means to examine the patterns from which our attitudes and behavior flow. Distinctions in language can set you free or entrap you. When we use the terms *dependency* or *female goodness,* we label ourselves. When we characterize other women as "tattles" or "witches," we are belittling not just an individual, but our own gender.

Author Émile Zola stated, "If you asked me what I came into this world to do, I will tell you: I came to live *out loud.*"

Expressing one's thoughts and feelings in language frees the spirit. Simply using the word *courage* to describe female energy perpetuates the feminine voice and sets a context for positive action. The sole reason to use the word *courage,* apply your definition of courage, and identify the twelve behaviors on the Source Wheel is to become a different kind of observer. By seeing things differently through the words you choose, you also are able to choose your behavior and to create a desired result. Language has great power to enable or discourage. Living *out loud* will galvanize your innate power to make courageous choices.

Living out loud *will galvanize your innate power to make courageous choices.*

PUTTING LANGUAGE TO WORK

You long to alter the context of your life, to break through and achieve your noblest aspirations. Yet in our society, few women are willing to identify themselves as courageous. Fewer still are willing to share that sense of courage with others. This reluctance is condoned by a society that rewards the courage exhibited through physically heroic feats, while the kinds of courage shown regularly by women go unnoticed. Exploring the unknown, confronting abuse, embracing faith, or choosing your own path are neither celebrated nor encouraged. Achieving a new perspective, both personally and collectively, often begins with language. Words are very powerful.

Consider love versus hate. Myra Bookman, Ph.D., professor of language and psychology at the University of Colorado at Denver, shared with me her understanding of the issues of hate speech and pornography. "Both are symbolic kinds of things that are not sticks and stones—they are not concrete, but they are very powerful in terms of race and gender. The idea that you can't just say whatever you want to someone implies that words can be as wounding as concrete, like throwing a stone. The law, examining the nuances of hate speech, agrees that words can indeed hurt you." This is an important point to consider when we rename our system of language, love, and consciousness.

Recently, a woman told me that her husband's illness had returned after a year in remission, and doctors gave him only months to live. When she finished sharing the pain of the situation I commented, "You are facing this imminent loss in a very courageous manner." She responded by telling me she really was not courageous, she was just doing what she needed to do—self-sacrifice for a loved one.

I shared this story with Dr. Bookman, who is familiar with this phenomenon in women. She had completed her postdoctoral work at Harvard University studying with Dr. Carol Gilligan, the foremost figure in researching the development of

159

morality in girls and women. Dr. Bookman told me
that in one stage of their moral development, girls
and women go through a self-sacrificial stage. The
stage has a cultural overlay that might be called "female goodness," which implies that a good woman
is a woman who sacrifices. She gave an example of
a woman saying, "No, don't worry about me, anything you want is fine." This conveys the idea that
the woman has no preferences or desires.

The label "controlling woman" usually connotes
a woman who expresses her preference or desire
rather than saying, "Whatever you folks want is
fine." Dr. Bookman feels this fits nicely into the
moral stages Dr. Gilligan talks about in her book *In
a Different Voice.* Dr. Gilligan discusses how the
self-sacrificial stage sometimes evolves into a more
mature personality. Dr. Bookman clarifies the point.
"Not to suggest that as women we get rid of this
other-centeredness and then become selfish, caring
only about ourselves. Rather, with caring and maturity, a woman does not need to sacrifice herself in
order to please others or get approval."

"... with caring and maturity, a woman does not need to sacrifice herself in order to please others or get approval."

The words a woman chooses to articulate her
needs and feelings help to determine her self-image
and the quality of her life. The words with which
we express ourselves can submerge and even sub-
jugate us into negativity, or they can elevate us into
love, enthusiasm, and joy. Words are a different vi-
bration from thoughts and feelings. As you learn to
listen deeply to other people, you will discover
tremendous differences in perception and be able
to appreciate the impact that these distinctions have
on communication.

In my courage coaching and training seminars I
listen to how a woman's internal experience is re-

flected in her language. The process requires me to hear how she describes herself—what she includes or leaves out. I also listen to metaphors she uses to define herself and those she chooses to describe her subjective world. Obviously, I must be careful not to place my own judgments on her experiences. For example, she may perceive a situation as a problem, while I see it as an exciting challenge.

One of the most important cultural shifts that has occurred within the past fifty years is that women have learned to use language to help them act from their convictions. As we embrace a new millennium, let us build on these gains.

BLASTING TO NEW LEVELS

Too often women see themselves through the eyes of those who devalue their contributions, and many blindly accept the myth that we are not supposed to direct our lives with courage. Allowing these concepts to flourish is to deceive ourselves as to our true value and potential. If we hold the assumption that we cannot change things, we will live our lives reacting to others instead of taking action ourselves. By reclaiming a courageous self-image that is based on concrete information, we can bring about positive change and move from resignation to the excitement of making self-rewarding choices.

By reclaiming a courageous self-image that is based on concrete information, we can bring about positive change . . .

If you watch TV soap operas or listen to the lyrics of popular songs on the radio, you are aware that suffering is glamorized. Spurned lovers croon about their broken hearts, and wronged spouses sink into a quagmire of despair. The implication is that broken hearts never heal. This creates a "role of expectations" that, unfortunately, some women choose as a model for their own behavior. These expectations

161

dictate that you react in the same way as the fictional characters—usually to your detriment.

A workshop called "The Language in Action" refined my understanding of the significance of the words we choose to describe our world. The program brochure read, "When we communicate effectively, we are able to intervene in and reshape the world in which we live." The coordinator told us we would learn basic distinctions between words, and that these distinctions would enable us to communicate more effectively and produce the results we were seeking in our personal lives and at work.

Our instructor, Julio Ollalla, played different styles of music—classical, country, rock, jazz, and rhythm and blues to reveal how our speaking is affected by our emotions. Different kinds of music evoke different emotions with which we perceive our world. Being aware of our emotions is essential when we attempt to change the way we use language.

FIXATION ON SUFFERING

Ask yourself: Is my suffering a private issue or am I making a case for suffering? Your language will guide you to the truth.

Dr. Caroline Myss, in *Anatomy of the Spirit*, writes that many people "have redefined their lives around their wounds and the process of accepting them. They are not working to get beyond their wounds."

Both the Enneagram (a typology of nine distinct personalities with different patterns of thinking, feeling, and acting) along with my interest in Buddhism (a religion that believes enlightenment can only be attained through courage) agree that there is suffering in human life and point out why and how we suffer. Both can be used to transcend our "wounded attachment" to allow us to focus on the fundamental aspects of our inner experience.

During periods of suffering, my voice of courage chooses words such as *pain* and *melancholy* to reveal my vulnerability. Recently, I was betrayed by someone I had trusted. A dear woman friend informed me that my partner was involved with another woman. I thanked my friend for her courage to speak the truth. The shock of this betrayal felt like I had been struck by lightning. I drew from my accrued allotment of courage to transcend my suffering and face the potential loss and truth of the situation.

Many times we have to be jolted by a shock before we can progress, because we are not committed to movement. We become stuck in one place, and we give ourselves labels. We say to ourselves, "I'm weak, I'm a loner, or I'm unlovable." Sometimes our beliefs may be unconscious. Emotional handicaps are common. Some are just more visible than others.

LANGUAGE IS ACTION

During my years of interviewing women for this book, conducting interpersonal skills training and courage coaching, I became aware of the importance of language. I learned how human beings interact with the world using language to describe their environment.

Language is a tool that can be used to release us from our fixation on suffering. Our descriptions govern our actions, and the meanings of certain words are deeply imprinted in our psyches. A reality of our culture—and most cultures around the

Language is a tool that can be used to release us from our fixation on suffering.

163

Courage *the heart and spirit of every woman*

world—is that women and girls are described as dependent, sacrificial creatures who must think of others before themselves.

Dr. Bookman feels that women are not to be blamed for subscribing to this kind of thinking. She said, "It is critical not to give the impression that the victim is being blamed, because our culture believes certain things about certain words. A woman who labels herself as dependent could actually be saying something wonderful and relational—that she desires closeness."

Dr. Bookman continues, "For over twenty years, our culture has struggled with using the word *Ms.* The idea of using Ms. to replace both Miss and Mrs. is a great example of how the meaning of these words is deeply imbedded in our national psyche. Mrs. has an underpinning attached to it."

The words we choose to use in conversation can be likened to a dance to our favorite music. Our words, body language, and emotions form a triangle through which we interpret the world around us. If we change the interpretation, we can shift the resulting behavior.

Consider the distinction between these three simple words: *discourage, courage,* and *encourage.* *Webster's* defines discourage as being deprived of courage, hope, or confidence; dispirit. Encourage means to inspire with courage, spirit, or confidence; to promote; foster. The definition of courage is bravery; facing and dealing with danger. In using these three words, moving in and out of the feelings of these words, we may be unaware of the profound influence of our interpretations on our behavior. A shift in interpretation yields a shift in behavior.

A shift in interpretation yields a shift in behavior.

Your words create your reality. When you speak,

you are "acting." Linguists technically call the process "performative acts." A word or words, sentences, or utterances are performances—meaning they make something happen. Promises, declarations, or words to persuade are performances that provoke action. The "action" provoked can be either physical or verbal. Dr. Bookman states, "The notion of words being actions or performing acts is very important, even now in linguistic studies." In the book *How We Do Things with Words*, J. L. Austin reveals how we automatically use words as a means to get people to do things for us, to endear ourselves to people, to make people like us, or to buy our products, with both positive and negative results.

WHEN YOUR "AUTOMATIC" BREAKS DOWN

Your actions are most effective when they are automatic and transparent. Tranparency means you are able to perform without having to reflect on the performance, such as when you drive your car. Driving is automatic and you are able to do it without thinking. While you are driving, you are in action, but not necessarily reflecting on the action. A "breakdown" occurs if you are suddenly jolted out of your "automatic" action—for instance, when you have a flat tire.

A breakdown is an occurrence that requires you to assess your circumstances in the moment. The breakdown offers a place for you to reflect and discover the cause of the incident. The Language in Action program revealed that in any country, in any language, when a flat tire occurs, the driver's reaction is usually "Oh, s_ _ _! Why me?" This "breakdown" of your automatic, effortless driving takes

165

you out of the transparency mode. You are your actions. A breakdown is a call to action—an opportunity to design your behavior instead of leaving it on automatic pilot.

Implementing courage requires you to choose a different action in the face of these interrupting breakdowns. Any habitual response is automatic and falls into consistent, unconscious patterns. Most people will resort to old patterns of past personal judgments. They'll ask themselves, "Why do things like this always happen to me?" or "Why am I cursed with such rotten luck?" These comments are the critical and judgmental thoughts that keep things the way they are, instead of brainstorming new possibilities. Considering different options leads to a sudden change in human behavior. Breakdowns create breakthroughs.

Implementing courage requires you to choose a different action in the face of these interrupting breakdowns.

Knee-jerk assessments make up the majority of our conversations and will anesthetize you. When we want to understand why something happened, such assessments are mostly useless and from the past. But analysis of them is necessary as we seek to establish new behavior patterns because they are a past declaration of who we are. And they are a strong force in keeping you the way you are, blocking future growth.

In the training session, Julio Ollalla said, "Assessments make up almost ninety percent of our speaking and are a key part of living together. But, assessments never have evidence. They are not binding, they may be entertaining, such as 'Look at her dress!' becomes a grounded assessment about how someone dresses. You do not question or ask, 'Why do you say what you say?' "

Avoiding Language-Induced "Breakdowns"

Breakdowns become less frequent when you design conversations that coordinate action. For example, you may ask someone to stop using words that put you down causing shame, blame, and diminishing self-esteem. In the moments of a language-induced breakdown, you will notice how your mood and emotions have changed—something fundamental has happened to you. With a breakdown come the old beliefs—the bigger the breakdown, the more overpowering the beliefs.

During times of breakdowns, I have trouble asking for help. I have asked myself why I feel that way. My fear stems from ungrounded assessments that I have come to believe about myself. For example, I feel I would be viewed as less independent if I asked for help. Without asking for help, I delay productivity, growth, or living in love. If I am to achieve a different outcome in my life, I must be willing and motivated to change my behavior and language. I can only enjoy a different outcome by choosing to be exposed. When I was betrayed, I gave myself permission to be vulnerable; I asked my friends to support me through a very difficult time. And that one small change in my previous assessment of myself made all the difference.

If I am to achieve a different outcome in my life, I must be willing and motivated to change my behavior and language.

New Language Habits Lead to Emotional Health

The action of speaking up makes something new happen. Speaking up and reaching out require the virtue of courage. Virtues define strength of character and healthy habits.

Our relationships are defined by the conversations we have or do not have with the people in our lives. You can determine the quality of your relationships by analyzing the conversation. Do you stay resentful toward your husband, telling others of his faults, or will you take a stand in courage and make a declaration to him? Ask yourself, "Am I using courage to declare my feelings?" "How do I create my conversation (dance) with someone?" and "Do I blame my mate and fail to generate a new context for our relationship?" (Casting blame on circumstances is strong in today's America.) "Or do I take responsibility to speak up to air the revealing truth?" The key behavior is to seek a place for "wonder" about what the behavior may be and listen for concerns. The idea that there is only one way to listen loses respect for listening.

Stephie, featured in a previous chapter, a national leader in women's business concerns and gender issues, comments:

"Women who do not use the word *courage* have lost their voice of courage. They have become captured or 'culturated' in the stereotype that women should not be courageous. Even if they step back to review their behavior and reclaim it later on, it is used in a limited way. They fell for the rap of being 'nice girls.' Perhaps when they become mothers and someone tries to mess with their kids, their courage will reignite."

Taking action fills your reservoir of courage and helps you to further find your voice.

Speaking Up Is Taking Action

Using words to clarify your position is taking appropriate action. Taking action fills your reservoir of courage and helps you to further find your voice. Language is the coordinator that brings us together and enables us to live together. Think of problem solving as a dialogue—with yourself or with another person.

Dialogue comes from the Greek *dia* and *logos* and translates literally as meaning "moving through." David Bohm, a physicist who conducted seminars on dialogue, says, "The ability to perceive or think differently is more important than the knowledge gained." Dialogue examines alternative views so the voice we carry within can discover a new view, a fundamental shift in perspective. Changing our perspective creates a distinct and more creative voice. Jill Mattuck Tarule writes in her essay, "Voices in Dialogue: Collaborative Ways of Knowing," that "out loud or silently, voice animates thinking, produces thought, and enables the thinker to stabilize and expand her thought."

"The ability to perceive or think differently is more important than the knowledge gained."

ENCOURAGING TRANSFORMATION

Words are a powerful tool for transformation. Consultant W. Edwards Deming stated, "Nothing happens without personal transformation." Transformations can and do occur as women alter the language that shapes their choices. Life is a continual process of becoming, of altering our being. Designing a new language to include the virtue of courage requires recognizing and acknowledging that language is action. Your words create your reality.

Life is essentially a learning experience. The product of learning is the capacity to produce an effective action. Undoing past learning may be painful. Perhaps you need to admit that you have been wrong in your previous approach. It is scary to admit you do not have the answer, and it is often embarrassing to have to ask questions. In school, we received good grades for good answers, not good questions. But a good therapist or coach understands the importance of asking questions, and invents "gaps" for you to ask bigger questions.

As a courage coach, I am interested in who you are becoming, not who you have been. In order to help you, a coach must see things from your perspective by observing the distinctions you make in the language you use to describe your world. A coach will challenge you to grasp new interpretations by building new distinctions in the words you use. For example, how do you communicate with a female friend on the telephone? Is it different in a work situation?

It takes conscious choice and effective action to dive into your heart and spirit to confront who you really are. We like to live in certainty. Uncertainty is not comfortable, but it is inevitable when you try to change.

Moving into a new awareness requires a promise to make necessary changes. A vow to a different approach requires action. The action is propelled when you consciously choose to use the behaviors of courage, as shown on the Source Wheel (see page 86). Applying the "faces of courage" to your canvas of life is critical to the development of your character. Virtues define the energy of your personality. When you feel this energy, the way you are in the world is not the same.

Courage is the portal of the heart.

Courage is the portal of the heart. Listen to your heart and choose to transform yourself through language.

CHAPTER TEN

CONSCIOUS CHOICE

Take your life in your own hands, and what happens? A terrible thing: no one to blame.

Erica Jong

WALKING YOUR OWN YELLOW BRICK ROAD

Transported from her home and her comfortable frame of reference, Dorothy embarked on a path of discovery that took her to the strange Land of Oz on the other side of the rainbow. After she inadvertently killed a wicked witch, she was thanked by a grateful "good witch," who awarded her the ruby slippers of the dead witch. Thus began her journey of self-revelation. Toward its end, she consciously faced and destroyed Oz's foremost villain, the Wicked Witch of the West. Finally unlocking the secret of personal fulfillment, Dorothy found that she was the only person who could get her what she desired most—a way back home. Her gift, the ruby slippers she had worn since the very beginning of her journey, was the key to get back to Kansas.

As you move down your personal yellow brick road, you are more likely to enjoy the journey as your range of choice increases. While it may not get you to Oz more quickly, the ability to make conscious choices will ensure that you are more mature and less naïve when you get there. A naïve woman

The only path toward consciousness is through the heart.

171

continues to make poor choices. The only path toward consciousness is through the heart.

Life is fundamentally a journey of consciousness, a state of growing awareness. William Jennings Bryan said, "Destiny is not a matter of chance; it is a matter of choice. It is not something to be waited for, but rather something to be achieved."

The beauty of developing awareness of human behavior patterns is that you can gain insight into your own way of seeing and responding to life's ups and downs. If you change your belief system and begin to live positively in uncertainty, you will face each day with the faith that you will be provided for in every way. Though coping mechanisms fluctuate from helpful to detrimental, they ultimately prevent us from creating our best selves. Let us hope that your desire for a new way of functioning is stronger than your desire to cling to old defenses. Your inner observer is ready and present when higher consciousness expresses itself.

I WANT WHAT I WANT

The greatest freedom in life is that of choice. The single most powerful investment you can ever make in life is in yourself. Your goal should be to add choices so you can define a different and positive pattern. This is the essence of growth. Establishing a constructive framework signals a useful course of action. Any increase in choice is an increase in opportunity. This makes choice a precious gift: the gift of independent thought and action.

This makes choice a precious gift: the gift of independent thought and action.

Carol S. Pearson writes in *The Hero Within*, "Most of us are slaves of the stories we unconsciously tell ourselves about our lives. Freedom begins the moment we become conscious of the plot line we are living and, with this insight, recognize that we can step into another story altogether. Our experiences of life quite literally are defined by our assumptions. We make up stories about the world and to a great degree live out their plots."

You alone are responsible for the design of your life. The choices you make become your road map. Once you develop a personal voice and move beyond conventional limited roles, you will develop the courage to act upon your personal purpose. By honing the specific behaviors of courage, you can transcend personal and societal barriers to succeed in whatever arenas you choose.

Designing a language of courage offers a whole new perspective of the choices available to you. In *Making Choices: Discover the Joy in Living the Life You Want to Lead*, Alexandra Stoddard wrote, "If we're willing to make difficult decisions that define our character, decisions that come straight from the heart, and we're also willing to take responsibility for the consequences of actions, we will discover that choice is what guides our personal destiny."

Being alive necessitates responding to the stresses and opportunities that come your way. When courage is consciously nurtured and strengthened, you are infused with the feminine energy to exert the power of choice. You can speak up, maintain your boundaries, and adhere to your beliefs. When courage is collectively harnessed, it becomes an instrument for the redefinition of self.

When courage is collectively harnessed, it becomes an instrument for the redefinition of self.

Every year, I jog the "Race for the Cure" to raise funds to fight breast cancer. When it first came to my hometown, the turnout was mediocre. Now the event is tremendously popular. The feeling generated by the women (and men) who support this cause is overwhelming. I seem to run a little faster now that the hope for a cure is shared publicly by so many. The collective energy defined the moment.

The goal of life is to invent and create, not to simply get by. It takes will and choice to break out of your behavior pattern. Stephen Covey states, in his book *The 7 Habits of Highly Effective People,* "Between stimulus and response, man has the freedom to choose. Within the freedom to choose are those endowments that make us uniquely human—self-awareness; imagination (the ability to create in our minds beyond our present reality); conscience (a deep inner awareness of the principles that govern our behavior, and a sense of the degree to which our thoughts and actions are in harmony with them); and independent will (the ability to act based on our self-awareness, free of all other influences). Once you have decided on your highest priorities, conscious choice takes over. It is the ability to act rather than to be acted upon."

Most of us sleepwalk through life. Dorothy and the Cowardly Lion fell asleep in the poppy field because the wicked witch had cast a poisonous spell on them. Most of us sleepwalk through life. We have fallen asleep to our essential self. In *The Wizard of Oz*, the good witch wakes up Dorothy and the Lion by making it snow so they can continue their journey to Oz. Change takes hard work. We must wake up and use conscious choice to follow our own yellow brick road.

YOUR FEMININE ENERGY:
FORCE TO BE RECKONED WITH

Our feminine energy is the power of our hearts and spirits to choose courage as a way of living. Choosing courage means not needing to be defined by the opinions of others or to gain the approval of others. Each journey begins by choosing new thoughts and attitudes and describing them through language.

Conscious choice requires taking responsibility for the experiences you create. You do many things out of habit. Sometimes the choices are little ones, such as deciding to honk your horn in irritation at another driver. Or they may be big ones, such as spreading malicious gossip about another person. These decisions affect the outcome of your life. Managing your choices is a full-time job.

Joseph Jaworski said, in *Synchronicity*, "I discovered that people are not really afraid of dying; they're afraid of not ever having lived, not ever having deeply considered their life's higher purpose, and not ever having stepped into that purpose and at least tried to make a difference in this world."

Discovering life's higher purpose requires courage. To see your purpose clearly is the gift of insight. Fulfilling that purpose requires even more courage.

"The freedom to choose brings with it the mantle of responsibility."

You may deceive yourself into believing that choice can be enjoyed without responsibility. William H. Nix writes, in *Character Works*, "The freedom to choose brings with it the mantle of responsibility. True freedom of choice does not exist without responsibility. Responsibility does not exist without a standard, or set of standards. It is the standard that creates the need for responsibility. The standard is a person's purpose."

Hopefully, all of us have some awareness of our specific purpose. To live on purpose means to not live by accident. One way to start the process of discovery is to simply ask yourself: "What is my purpose here on this earth?" and "What am I to do with my life?" The answers to these questions provide insight and help you discover your heart's desire.

You may experience a certain amount of fear when you discover your pattern of behavior in Chapter Seven, "Self-Discovery." When you realize your pattern of thinking and behavior, observe a breakdown, and design a new language, you should be motivated to change your choices. Learning is the catalyst for maintaining focus on your purpose.

All of which reminds me of a joke: How many therapists does it take to change a light bulb? Only one, but the light bulb has to be willing to be changed. To change your choices, consider calling *Courage is not* upon the virtue of courage. It takes courage to ex-*a tangible* perience life in a new and different way.

commodity. Courage is not a tangible commodity. Americans are addicted to material things: cars, houses, clothing, etc. Courage, however, is an inner-essence like love, creativity, and energy. Although you cannot buy it in a store, it is one of the most valuable possessions on earth. Without courage, we could never learn from our mistakes. Rita Mae Brown in *Rubyfruit Jungle* says the definition of insanity is doing the same thing, but expecting a different result.

Sue Patton Thoele, therapist and author of several books, shared with me in an interview, "No matter how much we learn the language of courage or how much we change our behavior, I am not sure we'll automatically be courageous one-hundred percent of the time. Fear is woven into the very fiber of our DNA—perhaps from the burning times (fifteenth- to seventeenth-century Europe)." Women were tortured during the burning times, and their courage was ripped away. Women were made to mistrust each other. She says, "But I do think one of the most courageous things we can do is to realize that we may have to re-choose and re-choose and re-choose to consciously act in new ways. Every once in a while we'll say, 'Hey, I just did that spontaneously.' Then we should congratulate ourselves, underscoring the behavior so that we'll be more likely to choose it again when presented with similar circumstances or feelings." With this approach, women can erase the mistrust that was imprinted into our souls through torment, and to trust each other again. To love each other is all there is time for.

To love each other is all there is time for.

At the moment you realize courage, you become fully identified with it. This connection reinforces your courage. Eventually, you will consciously feel the kinship, recognize the language, and realize you are living courageously.

I WANT MY DREAM BACK!

As a young girl, you had a dream about your future. But, perhaps the winds of fate blew you off course. The truth is, your life's journey depends on how closely your inner map matches the language of your outer reality. Surrendering some of your personality defenses such as pride, blame, humiliation, or greed, can facilitate change. The ultimate purpose of such surrender is to heal your judgments about yourself and see yourself anew. The fundamental goal: seek endless compassion, diminish old assessments, and use courage as a personal compass to direct your choices. Each day contributes in a meaningful way to the vision of your whole life. Manifesting your personal vision conveys courage.

Manifesting your personal vision conveys courage.

By owning and applying courage, women can make choices that lead to more satisfying lives as well as empower themselves to make a significant impact on the lives of their daughters, nieces, students, or other women in their lives. Recapturing the original meaning of courage—to act from one's heart—can strengthen your resolve in daily life. Thoele says, "The most courageous thing for us women to do is unearth our own authenticity with love, compassion, and gentleness. We need to learn to live gently with others and ourselves (although not wimpily). Doing so makes us stronger."

Making choices that expand our lives offers a richness of living—a different way of moving through life. It is the difference between living narrowly or broadly. Issues that arise in our lives do not announce they are coming. We must make choices. Embracing supportive virtues such as courage guides us down a path that allows us to live our own truth.

THE FACE OF COURAGE

Courage exhibits four distinct faces:

(1) **Courage is an invisible shield** of the heart offering us choices on how to create our lives. It can be called upon when facing any situation.

(2) **Courage is a self-generated perspective** available to each of us and provides the strength to take whatever action we desire.

(3) **Courage is a support** that strengthens our posture as we walk through life. Embracing its language provides a broad array of choices that allows us to create our lives in a different way.

(4) **Courage is a tool** wielded by the heart and drawn upon to approach the difficulties that arise in life.

LIFE'S CHALLENGES

The faces of courage change with the circumstances in our life. In Chapter Three, you read about Myrna's military experience in Desert Storm. In the military, she used courage as a shield to protect herself from the human suffering she witnessed. Once retired from the Army she faced a new challenge—motherhood. Again, she drew upon her courage to support her in this new challenge. While both responsibilities were different, fear and anxiety accompanied each. With motherhood, she constantly questioned herself: "Am I feeding my daughter right?" "Am I holding her correctly?" "Am I responding quickly enough when she cries?" and "Am I interpreting her cry right?" Myrna wanted to fulfill her daughter's needs, but her anxiety was extreme, particularly when the reason for the baby's crying could not be determined.

Myrna discovered that her courage was readily available to meet the challenge of motherhood. She said, "I could continue experiencing feelings of self-doubt, or I could be courageous and do the best I could." She coached herself to review the internal voice of self-doubt. "That's where the choice aspect comes in. Was I courageous or not? I would make the choice to be courageous—except for the days when I chose not to. On those days I would sit myself down and cry with the baby. But I did it consciously!" To be courageous or not is a choice. When you are at choice with courage, there is more of you.

When you are at choice with courage, there is more of you.

Myrna learned to recognize her emotions and their effect on her choices. She is able to identify the steps she needs to take to improve her situation, such as asking her husband for help. She knows her strengths and limitations. She has the determination and commitment to get a job done. These competencies are the building blocks to courage. Myrna says, "When I am courageous, I know what I want to do; I know there are obstacles, but my courage gets me through. That's where I pull from my intelligence, my motivation, and everything else." The two components of courage for her are self-awareness and choice.

While working full time, Myrna attends graduate school to complete a master's program in counseling, and does not make excuses for not being a perfect new mom. After all, it is a hard job. But she recognizes and calls upon her courage when the going gets tough. And she intends to structure a language that conveys and distinguishes courage for her daughter, because she believes that utilizing courage builds character.

Like Dorothy in Oz, we travel down the uncertain road of life, we are attentive to the lessons learned in each new experience, we can activate our innate feminine energy that enables us to face challenges and to respond appropriately in accepting new opportunities. We do not want to fall asleep in the poppy field and later wonder if we missed our higher purpose. George Konrad said, "Courage is only an accumulation of small steps." At the end of the journey, our words, our choices, and our actions reveal whether we followed our hearts.

At the end of the journey, our words, our choices, and our actions reveal whether we followed our hearts.

CHAPTER ELEVEN

COURAGE INTEGRATION

Remember always that you have not only the right
to be an individual, you have an obligation to be
one. You cannot make any useful contribution
in life unless you do this.

—Eleanor Roosevelt

RAISING YOUR DAUGHTERS TO BE COURAGEOUS

In Chapter Eight you read about women who struggled and improvised, combining different values in order to apply courage to their daily lives. Many of these women have been rejected or criticized for not conforming to stereotypical female roles regarding work or home, strength or vulnerability, caring or competition. Yet, they chose courageous individual action to achieve their goals. Each is living proof that projecting a new vision and creating new experiences leads to fulfillment.

As adult women, we have an incredible opportunity to stand in courage and guide our daughters . . .

Many of the women interviewed not only learned how to be courageous through their own experiences, they were encouraged by other women. Whether a grandmother, mother, sister, mentor, or friend, many women relied upon others to help them find their own voices. Once they discovered and voiced courage, they were able to pass this wisdom on to others, particularly their daughters.

As adult women, we have an incredible opportunity to stand in courage and guide our daughters

through their struggles during the normal matura-
tion process. Young girls today live in a completely
different world from the one in which we were
raised. Despite the women's movement, young girls
are having a harder time than ever before. This is
due in part to the expectations projected by the
media. Girls are also dealing with sexism, drugs,
gangs, AIDS, date rape, teen pregnancies, and high
levels of violence.

FEMININITY VERSUS FEMINISM

While girls are being raised to be assertive and confident, they are still unsure of the true meaning of
their femininity. They ask themselves, "If I am assertive, can I still be sensitive? Can I be delicate and
still be taken seriously? Does it diminish femininity
to be a feminist?" Feminism has not yet ensured
equal rights for men and women, so girls find it
confusing to differentiate between the two words.

In her graduate classes at the University of
Colorado, Dr. Bookman explains that feminism is
not about men versus women. "It is important to
distinguish between feminism and femininity and
that this is not a contest between men and women,"
she maintains. "Conventional femininity—dependency, lack of courage, or being other-oriented—as-
sumes self-sacrifice. There are many different
brands of feminism now and people are using the
plural 'feminisms.' Most, if not all, would like to
modify what the culture calls femininity. Even
though young girls are playing sports, I don't see a
clear indication that anything is really changing.
Women are not automatically feminists. They need
to be informed."

The dictionary defines feminist as "a doctrine advocating social, political, and economic rights for women equal to those of men; a movement for the attainment of such rights." Feminism is a way of life, not a label to be used to undermine the rights attained by women, such as flex-time and family-leave.

Dr. Bookman shared with me an amusing observation by feminist university instructors. When female students write a paper starting with "I am not a feminist but . . . ," they invariably believe in the basic tenet of feminism—the equality of the sexes. "The word just doesn't sit right with them," Dr. Bookman says. "Talk about language distortion. This is what these girls are reacting to—they want to be feminine in some sense, yet they are very confused about what it means. Feminism is not dead."

Yet the struggle continues. Consciousness-raising still works to catapult conscious choice. Mary Pipher writes, in *Reviving Ophelia: Saving the Selves of Adolescent Girls,* "Girls have long been trained to be feminine at considerable cost to their humanity. They have long been evaluated on the basis of appearance and caught in myriad double binds: achieve, but not too much; be polite, but be yourself; be feminine and adult; be aware of our cultural heritage, but don't comment on sexism. Another way to describe this femininity training is to call it false self-training. Girls are trained to be less than who they really are. They are trained to be what the culture wants of its young women, not what they themselves want to become."

"Girls are trained to be less than who they really are."

Femininity is not the sole province of women. As men allow themselves to embrace the power of the "feminine" in themselves and in our culture, traditional gender lines have become blurred.

Eventually, if the current trend continues, men, too, will understand and draw upon feminine courage to benefit the individual, the family, and the community at large.

Femininity is not the sole province of women.

HOW CAN GIRLS ACHIEVE THEIR FULL POTENTIAL?

It is especially difficult for girls to achieve their full potential because advice from older women is usually steeped in their own experiences and reflects the culture of their youth. Therefore, it is important for girls to adopt behaviors identified with courage.

Jan, the mother who faced abuse in Chapter Eight, used the word *courage* with her children for even little things. She related, "For my three kids, I use the word *courage* when they're getting ready to play football and soccer or to take tests. Sometimes I apply the word when they need to confront people, such as teachers. When my daughter Emily ran for class representative, I shared with her my feeling that it takes courage to run for an office because she is putting herself out there to be accepted or rejected."

Most of the women interviewed felt that parental support was critical in courage integration. When their daughters demonstrate a courageous act, these mothers give positive reinforcement. When courageous behaviors are encouraged, they are likely to be repeated.

Karen, first introduced in Chapter Three, asserted, "Not everybody has the ability to internally reinforce their own courageous behavior. Parents and teachers need to openly identify the courageous acts and reinforce them positively. When I was growing up, my mother *en*couraged me and provided me with specific examples of other courageous actions. Many times I did not realize that my choices were courageous. I resigned from my high school sorority because I disagreed with the treatment of some of the less popular girls. Usually, I did not think that I was particularly courageous. I am very grateful for my mother's insight."

Girls need this kind of *en*couragement. Having a strong family model or mentor builds a foundation of support that allows a young woman to step out of the comfort zone and identify with courage in a more enlightened way in her daily life. Without this, she may feel confined to the traditionally understood definition of courage—heroic feats of daring, such as dragon slaying or fighting in a war.

Having a strong family model or mentor builds a foundation of support . . .

START WHEN THEY ARE YOUNG

Dr. Jane L. Bilett, child psychologist and practicing therapist specializing in women's issues, believes parenting does not have to be haphazard; it can be purposeful and intentional. Dr. Bilett, whose career spans thirty years, was cognizant of the impact her actions and responses would have on the future development of her two children, a son born when she was thirty-five, and a daughter three years later. Dr. Bilett says, "When my daughter J.J. was six months old she was able to 'elephant walk' up a slide. I could have taken her off the slide or told her 'no, no,' sending a negative message that such attempts were too dangerous. At nine months she walked, and at eighteen months she tiptoed high beams and jumped off the diving board. She discovered in each one of her challenges that she could accomplish whatever she wanted by taking risks, getting feedback, and refining her strategy. The developmental message she connected with from me was that overcoming obstacles and learning skills was no big deal."

Dr. Bilett shared with me that she continued to encourage her daughter's independence and self-respect. When J.J. was six years old, boys at her school made a game of lifting up girls' dresses on the playground. Dr. Bilett says, "I made a big fuss with the principal about her being able to physically protect herself, in whatever way felt comfortable to her, whether it be verbal or physical. J.J. thought she would get in trouble with her teachers if she kept her boundaries by saying 'no' to someone who tried to pull up her dress or responded physically." Mother and daughter had the courage to confront the principal about their convictions that J.J. had the right to protect herself in any way she deemed necessary.

Dr. Bilett does not worry excessively about J.J. as a teenager at parties. She believes that her daughter has known since she was six years old that she can do anything she needs to do to protect herself. "A sixteen-year-old is better able to protect herself if she developed that skill at six. If a little boy pinches a girl on the arm, the girl (or woman) needs the courage to confront that abuse and say it is not okay, because later it becomes a pinch on the ass." When a girl develops a positive perception of herself at a young age, she is better able to consciously make healthy decisions.

Risk-taking and hurdling obstacles should begin at an early age.

The goal is to integrate each characteristic (manifestation) of courage with purpose. Risk-taking and hurdling obstacles should begin at an early age. Both are prerequisites for being strong and determined. Dr. Bilett's daughter has grown into a very self-assured young woman who plays sports, runs for student council, and goes on five-day backpacking trips as well as to homecoming dances. Dr. Bilett says, "You don't get a flower without preparing the soil, planting the seed and weeding the garden."

"An incredible number of women have no sense of who they are or what matters to them."

Dr. Bilett related that in her practice she sees a noticeable absence of courage in women. She says, "An incredible number of women have no sense of who they are or what matters to them. The quintessential 'Southern Belle' type that I am seeing in therapy can go to a tea wearing gloves, be a gracious hostess, or charm other guests at a cocktail party, but she is defined by her performance of these social duties. She meets other people's needs beautifully, but doesn't know her own needs or who she is. She is the moon to their sun; she has no light of her own."

Such women require a lot of courage to develop their self-esteem. By age thirty-five, many become depressed. Because their sense of real self-worth was never developed when they were younger, they are acutely unhappy with the person they have become. Dr. Bilett says, "Self-esteem is the opposite of 'what will the neighbors think?'" In her practice, Dr. Bilett has explained many times to her patients, "Girls raised in an environment where only surface values are admired never receive the character-building training that develops courage; so how can they have it automatically as adults?"

BUCKING A CULTURE THAT STILL EXPECTS WOMEN TO BE SUBMISSIVE

The ultimate goal in defining or understanding courage as a genderless virtue is to place value on behaviors other than death-defying acts, behaviors that are typically viewed as feminine, such as raising children. This accomplished, men and women can live interdependently in ways that value and honor each other.

A scene from the Academy Award–winning movie *Titanic* illustrates the inequality between the sexes during the early part of the 1900s. An anxious mother is determined her daughter will marry a wealthy young man so that both mother and daughter can resume the lifestyle they enjoyed when the "man of the house" was alive. The mother sternly tells her headstrong daughter, "We are women; our choices are never easy." Women were taught to seek husbands who were older, taller, richer, and more intelligent. *Titanic* and *The Wizard of Oz* were both popular in their time. Both movies discourage women from being the archetype of the Goddess. Perhaps the remake of the *Titanic* was to remind us—do not go after what we want!

Dorothy depicts a feminine young girl, perfectly dressed, living in Kansas on a rickety old farm. From the very beginning of the movie, she is compassionate and worried in an appropriate self-imposed manner. She demonstrates her frustration about Toto not following the rules. Dorothy stomps her foot and says with exasperation, "Oh!" She struggles throughout the movie between being independent or dependent on the men around her. She even thinks the ultimate power belongs to the Wizard (another male figure).

Throughout Dorothy's journey in Oz, her image portrays a damsel in distress, or a girl helplessly lost in the woods. Dorothy's role in the movie was the model of femininity for an earlier generation of women. Each time I watch the movie I become more aware of the gender distinctions. All the companions, including Toto, are males. There is only one "good" witch and she appears in the beginning, the middle, and the end of the movie. The other key female roles are a source of harm to Dorothy.

One of Dorothy's first actions of affirming strength is when she meets the Cowardly Lion on the Yellow Brick Road. When the Lion frightens Toto, Dorothy sweeps Toto up and slaps the Lion on the nose and tells him to pick on someone his own size. While she can stick up for others, she does not recognize her own sense of self; in fact, she is actually startled at her assertive response.

Later in the movie, the wicked witch is holding Dorothy prisoner in the castle and Toto escapes by running out a window. Crying, Dorothy realizes she is doomed to die; yet, she remains concerned for everyone else (self-sacrificial) and screams to her precious Toto to run for safety—at least he will be spared.

Dorothy is no Xena when she accidentally splashes the pail of water on the witch to save the Scarecrow from burning. The message of the movie is, "If your intentions are good, then that is fine, but if you are being too strong and forceful, that is not good. Strength should only prevail by happenstance or luck." Keep in mind the time when this movie was made, the 1930s. This was a time when men still could not accept a self-confident demeanor from Dorothy. Her job was to support all the males on the journey by being the archetypal woman.

Even at the end of the journey in Oz, Dorothy continues to build up her three companions' egos. She coddles Scarecrow and says specifically to him, "Without you, I am totally lost." Dorothy's intelligence, courage, and unfulfilled emotions are repressed. All she frets about is whether Auntie Em is sick or hurt.

Dorothy would have made a worthy wife in her time because a "good woman" knew her place: there's no place like home. To stay out of trouble, Dorothy learned several important lessons: never again believe she knows it all, never try to take charge, and never show independent thinking by running away.

The theme of *The Wizard of Oz* does not represent modern woman. While the movie is still popular today, we should say to ourselves, "That was then and this is now."

MEN SUPPORTING WOMEN

I asked several women how they could specifically encourage men to be supportive of them, either during difficult times or when they were authenticating the feminine energy of courage.

Dr. Myra Bookman, a professor of linguistics and psychology feels, "Choose carefully the men that you relate to. This is harder to do in the workplace. Men and women hold deeply ingrained ideas from their culture. There's not much one person can do to change that except pay lip service. The best strategy would be to let people know when they are saying something that has a significant meaning. Let them know that you are hearing something that they are not necessarily aware they are saying. For example, when a man refers to a grown woman as girl or gal. In the same context, a woman would not call a mature man a boy. So inform people why these things are important. Unfortunately, if somebody has deeply imprinted values about what women ought to be and what men ought to be, you have a big problem on your hands. This requires the courage to speak up and hold your boundaries."

"This requires the courage to speak up and hold your boundaries."

Dr. Jane Bilett, a therapist specializing in women's issues, believes, "An interesting concept is that women have a harder time being courageous when dealing with men. It's easier for women to speak with women about courage than with men. Our culture still projects the idea that women should 'take the back seat.' What may be more powerful is for fathers to consciously choose to encourage their daughters to be courageous. The mother can request the father to be involved in the early development of courage in daughters. Otherwise, the most essential thing we need to do as women is to support one another, unite in a conscious way to encourage, augment, and congratulate each other on the courage we show. Men need to accept the choice of a woman as the choice of an equal.

"One of the ways I shared the notion of courage was to read feminist fairy tales to my daughter," Dr. Bilett continues. "A father or significant male-figure could do similarly to a daughter or niece. One of my favorite books is a collection called *Womenfolk and Fairy Tales*, edited by Rosemary Minard. The book focuses on girls and women who are propelling forces, such as Molly Whuppie, who takes a giant to task. The collection covers different cultures. All the women are strong, bright heroines who do cool things—no downtrodden Cinderellas scrubbing floors here! What we read to our daughters is very important. It can send a message of 'I don't have to get permission to be courageous. I do not need to seek a man's approval; approval must come from within me.' Real courage comes from the magic within."

Dr. Catharyn Baird, a professor of business, teaches law and ethics, public policy, and gender issues and attitudes toward business. Dr. Baird is also a wife and mother with one daughter, a stepdaughter, and a son and stepson, all of whom she raised to be feminists. She comments, "Culturally, women are taught to defer to men. Even those of us who are aware of this tendency, often give information to the significant men in our lives in the form of a question, rather than engaging in a conversation as an adult to an adult. The tendency to ask rather than tell is very subtle.

"Real courage comes from the magic within."

"A few years ago, I made the decision to move my career emphasis from teaching to writing. Rather than discussing with my husband the decision, I began to strategize what the change would mean in my life. I asked him whether he thought I was a good writer and whether I had anything to say. He looked at me like I was nuts and dutifully confirmed my ability. Two days later (after being annoyed at his simplistic dismissal of my question), I asked the real—the vulnerable—question, 'Will you be there for me while I go through this scary change in career?' The answer was very different. 'Yes, he would be pleased to support me through the process of learning to write for the public.' Our relationship was strong enough to support me on a new journey."

Dr. Baird continued, "If we learn to share our hopes and our dreams from a position of ownership rather than seeking permission from men, either actively or implicitly, men will not be confused as to whether we are seeking support and affirmation for our choices or guidance and permission."

". . . learn to share our hopes and our dreams from a position of ownership rather than seeking permission from men . . ."

Amy Matthews (fictitious name), is a thirty-year-old lawyer currently staying at home to care for her toddler daughter. "I believe that men can help women by sacrificing their own goals in order to support their spouses. I was unhappy as a trial attorney in a large firm. Sometimes I would close my office door and just cry. Gender relations at work were twenty years behind corporate America. Two female attorneys sued the firm for sexual harassment. Fortunately, my husband, John, encouraged me to leave the job. With his support, I was able to summon the courage to take the risk and quit.

"After searching for a position in a big law firm, I realized I no longer wanted to trade a Mercedes for the nights with my child. John's encouragement gave me the courage to follow a different career. He adjusted his dream of being the stay-at-home parent and worked hard as a computer contractor to support our family. I think most women do not have such supportive men in their lives to bolster their courage. I hope my daughter can learn from her father's example that women have as much right as men to follow their dreams. Perhaps she will live in a society where marriages are truly equal partnerships, and there are no gender gaps."

THE CHALLENGE OF THE WORKPLACE

Not so long ago, women's work was defined by their bodies: they bore children and were generally considered the weaker sex. If they had to earn a subsistence wage, they worked as household help, nurses, teachers, and governesses, and in some areas, as sewing-machine operators. Eventually, women became typists, secretaries, and telephone operators.

World War II promoted women by necessity into defense plants to replace men called into the service of their country. When the war ended and the men came home, women tried briefly to go back to being "just housewives," but, having received a taste of the satisfaction that comes from earning their own money—being in control of their own lives—they quickly became dissatisfied with confinement to the home. That dissatisfaction, coupled with reliable birth control, soon sent them rushing pell mell into the working world (and divorce rates soared).

But the workplace, too, had its drawbacks. Women earned considerably less than men for comparable work—and they still had to carry the entire load of running the household and caring for the children. Soon the women's movement and affirmative action laws demanded that doors to the corporate world be opened to women, and that the pay be more equitable. In the sixties and through the seventies, though women earned only fifty-nine cents for each dollar earned by a man for comparable work, women had gained a solid toe-hold. In the eighties, women's pay rose to seventy cents for every dollar earned by a man for similar work, but there still remained a "glass ceiling," an invisible prejudice against women that kept them from top management positions.

When the high-tech industry blossomed more than twenty years ago, women thought their successes would increase. Esther Dyson writes in "The Sound of the Virtual Voice" that "it hasn't turned out that way. With a few exceptions, women still have a tough time making it into management. We're still socialized to look to men for leadership. Power is based not on performance alone, but on presence and perception of managerial personality. In business, women still face a different code than men."

Although it is true that women have come a long way in recent years, inequities remain. Bridled by our different status, we still seek full equality. Nancy Ramsey, who coauthored *The Futures of Women* with Pamela McCorduck, shared some of the findings in her book. The findings calculate a future using 1970 as a benchmark for change. In 1999, fewer than three percent of senior managers at the nation's largest corporations were women. "At this rate, it will be the year 2270 before women and men are equally likely to be top managers of major corporations," Ramsey says, "and Congress could not expect to achieve equality between women and men before the year 2500. Men represent the same story of incremental progress in pay levels, while women today still earn seventy-five cents per dollar earned. This is no glide path to equality for women. This is a glacier."

" . . . it will be the year 2270 before women and men are equally likely to be top managers of major corporations . . ."

WOMEN'S TRADITIONAL PROFESSIONS ARE NO BETTER

In order to compare women's places in corporate America with traditional professions of women, I interviewed Edna Cadmus, Ph.D., a nurse executive in a medical center on the East Coast. While talking with her, it dawned on me that the nursing profession is one of the largest professions, like teaching or secretarial work, that is comprised mostly of women.

Cadmus, who has been in the nursing profession for more than twenty-three years, told me that the medical environment is constantly and rapidly changing; yet the dynamics of the environment are not keeping pace with these changes. Hospitals tend to be organized in a hierarchical manner that supports a bureaucratic or mechanistic method of operation. This masculine order contradicts the nurturing nursing profession of predominately females. Like the pull of a rubber band, the nature of the institution requires a give and take between these two opposing points of view. Anger rises when the nurses are stretched to the limit. The nurses perceive they are the only ones who have to give emotionally. Yet, in that setting, anger is not considered an acceptable female emotion. Many nurses do not know how to effectively dispense with this anger and become emotionally drained.

. . . anger is not considered an acceptable female emotion.

After discussing my research with Cadmus, I faxed her the Source Wheel (see page 86). She told me in a follow-up interview that the Behaviors of Courage could provide a valuable tool to nursing professionals. Cadmus says, "In the volatile health-care environment, a nurse can choose not to compromise her values by recognizing her courage to be strong and determined. Peer support is a valuable asset if a nurse is willing to share her vulnerabilities. The courage to take risks requires her to open herself up to criticism and conflict. The emotion of anger can be debilitating over time, the courage to speak up can reduce or eliminate this frustration."

Cadmus identified that these same issues were also found at the executive level. As women advance within the hospital organization, most of their peers are men. She said, "At this level, the nurse executive is frequently viewed differently because she is a woman and a nurse. To retain personal convictions requires the courage to overcome fear of failure and lack of acceptance by colleagues. Speaking up in a male-dominated structure can be risky, and can even result in failure. Critical at this stage is the ability not to change or compromise her core values. I believe courage comes from within one's heart—it's what all nurses and women have naturally."

"To retain personal convictions requires the courage to overcome fear of failure and lack of acceptance by colleagues."

ALL'S FAIR IN LOVE AND WAR

How can we harness courage to be a part of every woman's willful energy? The need for this unified power reminds me of my dear friend Catharyn's favorite play, *Lysistrata*, by Aristophanes. Lysistrata, an Athenian woman, summoned all of the women and their warring neighbors to Athens to campaign for peace. Their strategy was to refuse to bed with their husbands until the war ends and peace is declared throughout the region. Catharyn remarked, "The play had several delightful components: convincing all the women to go without sex and refuse their husbands; dealing with the unrequited desire and trickery of the men; and the ultimate prize of peace." This is not to champion withholding sex to get what you want. However, the story reveals what can happen if women take control over the areas of their lives where they do have power to change the course of history.

. . . the story reveals what can happen if women take control over the areas of their lives where they do have power . . .

FOSTERING COURAGE IN THE WORKPLACE

Women forging the twenty-first century must master the core competencies of courage in order to advance in the workplace. Retired Professor Mary Daly, a feminist philosopher and theologian who barred men from her classroom at Boston College, called the feminine energy *gynergy* (from gynecology). Forced to retire at age seventy for using separatism in the classroom, Dr. Daly lost what she called "women-space." Today, work equality requires figuring out how to be a fully present woman in a mixed gender workplace or classroom. That way we can increase our consciousness as well as our conscience about these things.

Dr. Judith Briles, an author and speaker specializing in women's issues in the workplace, has spent years researching the prevalence of sabotage by co-workers. Her most recent book, *Woman to Woman 2000: Becoming Sabotage Savvy in the New Millennium,* finds that women are more likely to sabotage other women, rather than men.

In a telephone interview, Dr. Briles stated that she believed that sabotage by other women in the workplace can keep women from harnessing courage. She said, "One of the issues that happens with women comes from childhood conditioning. I call these conditionings 'momisms.' An example of a momism is the admonition: 'Don't fight.' Later in life, perhaps at work, women tend to view confronting someone who may be deliberately hindering them as an offshoot of fighting, possibly because the confronted person goes on the defense. Fearing such a response, most women remain silent, giving the female saboteur license to continue her destructive behavior. Such frustrating reactions on the part of both women will reflect or reduce the wronged woman's courage quotient."

". . . frustrating reactions on the part of both women will reflect or reduce the wronged woman's courage quotient."

Dr. Briles also suggested that applying courage at work meant that when sabotage behavior is activated, it is essential for a woman to speak up, and express her concerns. The victim should state how she wants the behavior altered and perhaps demand that it discontinue immediately.

Today, women make up more than 50 percent of the workforce. Most working women want careers as well as a husband and children. Every woman must make that choice for herself. But, not so long ago, a woman in certain cultures could be severely punished by male relatives for refusing to marry the man her family selected for her. Now most women have the choice to mate by preference and they can choose to do "men's jobs."

Now is the time for women to finally claim the prize of full self-actualization, "over the rainbow," where the first step is always the most courageous. The Source Wheel reveals the faces of courage that distinguish each unique behavior of courage so that women can reclaim the heart and spirit that were once the vital essence of the Goddess period.

CONCLUDING THOUGHTS

Courage Is the Rainbow

No doubt if *The Wizard of Oz* represented real life, Dorothy would be grown up by now, living in a small city, happily married, and content baking chocolate-chip cookies for her children and husband. Her memory of being awestruck by the splendor of the rainbow in the Land of Oz would be long forgotten. She would be transformed into the lifestyle meant for a woman of her time.

I am blessed to live in an area that frequently displays double rainbows. Recently, I saw a magnificent one. People were standing outside gazing in astonishment at the vibrant hues that arched through the sky. Fall was in the air and the last of the late blooming flowers were overflowing the flowerbeds. Many thoughts filled my mind as I gazed at nature's magnificent creation.

The day I saw this rainbow, I was finishing the long journey of writing my first book. It had taken many years—much longer than I had anticipated. Exposing my heart on the journey created a cathartic healing. I connected my quest with the sacred feminine within me—within all women. The transformative power of my feminine energy reawakened my mother-goddess, the divine mother that beckons every woman to save the world from destruction.

I have lost my inner grounding many times during my life. As I reflected on the majestic rainbow, I thought of the mythic figure Iris. This beautiful woman, a messenger of the gods, traveled the rainbow linking the earth with other worlds. Diana Wells writes about the iris with its trinity of petals dedicated to the Virgin Mary in *100 Flowers and How They Got Their Names*, "She [Iris] escorted souls along her iridescent bridge to another life, and she often joined the thoughts of gods and men. She was the longed-for connection to those whom we love intensely, but who are suffering without our awareness."

FORGET-COURAGE-NOT

Women are like the flowers that echo the spectrum of colors in the rainbow—the many different varieties, each impressive and unique in her own way. When I pondered about my love of flowers and rainbows, I remembered one of my favorite blooms—forget-me-nots. Associated with bravery, they come from the borage family in the Middle East. The ancient Celtic warriors drank borage-flavored wine to give them courage. In medieval paintings, the Virgin Mary's robe is almost always the celestial blue of the forget-me-not. Blue forget-me-nots are often used to decorate Valentine cards as an expression of love and caring.

These small but significant flowers symbolize the main message in this book: every woman needs to forget-courage-not as she travels her yellow brick road. On her journey to reclaim heart and spirit, every woman's courage can lie coiled in bud and then miraculously uncoil as courage expands within her, bringing her into gorgeous blossom.

Collectively, women are the fierce force that can awaken world consciousness. Our salvation lies in living the truth of our hearts and spirits by harnessing our courage.

In this new millennium, women are birthing a divine feminine energy to reclaim the forgotten heart and spirit of every woman.

Every woman needs to forget-courage-not as she travels her yellow brick road.

Books Recommended by the Courageous Women

We do not recognize that the fierceness
of the lioness is as right and beautiful
as the roar of the lion.

Marianne Williamson
A Woman's Worth

Alexis Ralston: I loved *Women Who Run with the Wolves* by Clarissa Pinkola Estes. As I "wised up" over the years, the poignancy of the stories grew on me, just as the fascinating and affirming stories in *Courage: The Heart and Spirit of Every Woman.* In my thirties, my life mirrored the stories in *Wolves.* I was a single mom with two girls, trying to make a living in man's world—commercial real estate. Trying to be the Super Mom, swimming in triathlons and exercising my jaws with men, I had no time to resonate with Clarissa's message. I am now in my forties, my daughters are in college, and I have simplified my life. Now, as highlighted in *Wolves,* the courage to remember the everyday conscious acts of self-love, acceptance, laughter, compassion, kindness, and curiosity is deeply appreciated.

Angela: I read the Bible often, particularly when I have a bad day. I also love Danielle Steel's books because every woman in her books has survived something and overcome obstacles.

203

Anne: The Bible has had a big impact on me. Reading it makes me stop, think, and figure out how to apply it to my life.

Bonnie Barnes: The most significant book I have read is the Bible. In addition, M. Scott Peck's *The Road Less Traveled* maps how to bring our entire lives into complete balance. It was wonderfully inspiring and it was my life. I felt like I had been on that road my entire life and I didn't know anybody else was on the road with me. I no longer felt alone.

Candace: My favorite book is *The 7 Habits of Highly Effective People*, by Stephen Covey. It reminds me to be well-rounded. And, of course, the *Course in Miracles* philosophy saved my life.

Carol Francis Rinehart: The book that had an impact on my life the most was the novel *Beloved* by Toni Morrison. Sethe, the female protagonist is a slave woman who, in order to keep her children from being sent back to their prior slave owner, decides to take their lives in order to "free" them. I was deeply moved by this character. She was raped, whipped, tortured, and brutalized; yet, against all odds, her courage, strength, and convictions made her take a stand to be the sole supporter of whatever was left of her family. While her exterior was aloof, hard and mean, her interior soul was feminine and maternal. In the end, she was vulnerable; her spiritual "all-mother self" encouraged her to find the grace to love herself. Finally, with that discovery, she was set free. I also endured sexual abuse, beatings, and verbal degradation from my father;

yet, I developed a facade of hardness to survive. With the help of God, what made me "free" was my ability to own courage, invite vulnerability, and recover the grace and gratitude to love myself. Now, I fully love others.

Carol Veatch: A book that I read and reread is *The Tao of Pooh* by Benjamin Hoff. This is a sweet book that seems to put things back into perspective for me. Pooh "just is"! The message reminds me to slow down, simplify, and be kind.

Cene Backus: When reading the Christian Science textbook, I am inspired by *Science and Health with Key to the Scriptures* by Mary Baker Eddy. The Bible has also been instrumental in my life as a source of inspiration and an answer to whatever challenges I must face. Regular study of these two books prevent, as well as cure, problems of all kinds.

Danielle: *Necessary Losses* by Judith Viorst was important to me as I left home for the first time. I faced so many changes when I moved from a small town in Michigan to New York to be a nanny. This book had an impact on me because it clarifies the illusions we all have as we attempt to become our full, true self and grow in our relationships. The examples of loss and growth hit every nerve. It also shed light on the need for strength and the courage to live life to its fullest. Life is full of loss and gain, painfully at times and joyfully at other times.

Debra Heskin: The Bible has had a big impact in my life. I can put the book down for a few years then pick it up and it's amazing what a verse will say to me. I have a strong belief that no matter what I'm going through, good or bad, all I have to do is open the Bible and it will say something to help me. Another book that had a huge, positive impact on me was *The Power of Positive Thinking* by Norman Vincent Peale. The book helped me look at life very differently. What I learned is that it is all about me. If I am down in the dump, it is up to me to get me out. If it's work related, it will take me to make a difference. Just finding the positive side in everything helps me grow.

Diane: *The Battered Woman's Survival Guide: Breaking the Cycle* by Jan Berliner-Statman and *Getting Free: A Handbook for Women in Abusive Relationships* by Ginny Nicarthy are the two books that inspired me to take action. They helped me open the door to seek a life beyond what I had known in my abusive relationship. It gave me hope; but even more than that, it gave me my life back. When reading these books, I came to know that I was not the only person in an abusive relationship. I came out of my seemingly hopeless, isolated state and found the courage to seek help. I read about other women's experiences that paralleled my own and drew from their courage.

Donna Baumer: Over twenty years ago, I read *My Mother, Myself* and *The Daughter's Search for Identity* by Nancy Friday. When I finished reading these books, I realized I was more like my mother than I wanted to admit. I realized that the mistakes my mother had made weren't mistakes at the time. She did what she thought was right for us kids, such as keeping certain truths from us. Years later, I came to realize that my mother did the best she could and that I would probably have made the same choices. This showed me how to do deep soul searching in myself, which allowed me to understand my mother and why she did what she did. I also enjoyed *Mind Traps: Change Your Mind, Change Your Life* by Tom Rusk. In my thirties, I realized I lacked self-esteem and that I was going through life in the same old pattern. This book pumped me up and the self-help suggestions motivated me to go back to school. I gained self-esteem, which allowed me to stand up for what I wanted instead of letting everyone else run my life. This revealed the different self-inflicted attitudes we may have and not even know about. This book offered new thinking patterns.

Eva Ortiz: My favorite book is the Bible. My convictions stand on being honest in life. As a child, I liked to hear biblical stories (Noah's Ark, the flight out of Egypt, Moses, etc.) as well as *Grimm's Fairy Tales*. As an adult, I like reading the Old Testament and comparing it with the New Testament. The process has guided me in all my teachings of "religion," such as catechism classes and for my own life. Proverbs and the Psalms are two of my favorites, both written by wise men who had tried everything under the sun and found it to be "nothing" in the end—so all praise went to God! Daily reading of the New Testament gives me the peaceful existence I so enjoy today. Psalm 145:13 is a verse to cherish!

Goldie Cohn: I loved *Moby Dick* by Herman Melville because of the challenge; the Ibsen plays because of their sadness; Hemingway's works; and John Grisham's books because I became fascinated with legal affairs; and so many other books and magazines, including autobiographies.

Jan: One of the best books I have ever read was by Wally Lamb called *She's Come Undone.* The book represents an example of courage. The main character is a woman. The book follows her life from about three years old to her forties and reveals all of her hardships and problems. She was abused by a neighbor, her mother was put in an institution, her parents divorced, and she was ridiculed for being obese. Even after trying to commit suicide, she overcame all the obstacles to find happiness—the happiness she had searched for her whole life. It was hard for me to believe it was fiction because for me it was so real. I had been knocked down and on my knees, and started all over again. Her courage and choices made her crawl again, just like me. I dusted myself off and walked away. I felt it was too bad she didn't identify courage early in her life; maybe she would have made different choices sooner.

Jennifer: I do not have a book that has made an impact on me, but I do have a poem called "If" by Rudyard Kipling. It is about keeping our patience—another critical virtue.

Joan Badzik: Many strong women have had an impact on my life, but none more significantly than the women I have found in the Bible. In the Old Testament book of Esther, Queen Esther is a profile in human courage. Here is a Jewish woman whom God positioned with great favor as a queen to a foreign king. God used her to uncover a plot to obliterate the captive Jewish people; Jews today still celebrate the Feast of Purim in honor of her courage. Another biblical woman of incredible courage is Hannah, found in 1 Samuel 1:2–21. Here we find a woman not able to conceive a child, and well acquainted with sorrow, rejection, and humiliation. Instead of giving up, she took her brokenness, sorrow, and grief to God in passionate prayer (1 Samuel 1:11–19). She courageously sought her Maker and He granted her prayer request. A woman of passion and prayer, her faith in God birthed through her a prophet and judge to Israel: Samuel.

Jody: *The Courage to Heal: A Guide for Women Survivors of Child Sexual Abuse* by Ellen Bass gave me a lot of support and helpful insight and was personally fulfilling.

Judy Zerafa: *Think and Grow Rich* by Napoleon Hill was the first book I read in the self-help genre. It gave me clear directions on how to get started on self-improvement. *The Greatest Salesman in the World* by Og Mandino touched my soul. It allowed me to see that every act I take has a spiritual consequence and that every professional/career decision should be made from the standpoint of spiritual well-being.

Karen McGee: *The Diary of Anne Frank* by Anne Frank inspires courage because of the age and dire straits of the author. The courage she demonstrated was at the highest level. Any of us can demonstrate courage in our daily lives, but we don't have to demonstrate it at the level she did. It makes it easier to draw on our own courage when we think of the courage Anne Frank showed during that horrible time. To me, the highest form of courage is facing death and hopeless situations with spirit and optimism. That's what Anne Frank demonstrated.

Kay: *Man's Search for Meaning* by Viktor Frankl left a permanent impression on me primarily because it taught me that any courage I might gain resides in me. Regardless of the conditions or situations that I am facing, I ultimately choose the way I respond to those conditions or situations. The author taught me that courage is a choice.

Laurie Graves: The most important book in my life was *When Enough Is Enough* by David Augsburger. This book is fascinating because it bundles all the topics I love: philosophy, anthropology, sociology, poetry, and psychology.

Lila: The book that had the most impact in my life was *Diary of a Fat Housewife* by Rosemary Green. While the book has not made me lose weight, it is about the diary of a woman struggling with being overweight. The most profound impact of the book was the complete honesty. I appreciated that aspect. I do crazy things as an overweight woman and the author was able to share honest things, such as how quickly we get into a swimming pool.

Linda Betz: In the mid-seventies, I entered the workforce bombarded with books from the feminist front. A book that stuck with me was Gail Sheehy's *Passages.* The book focuses on chronological stages in our lives and the challenges that go with them. And, like this book, it was peppered with actual vignettes from women's lives. I learned several things from the book: expect some of these things to happen to you during your lifetime, learn from the successes/failures these women experienced, expect to handle crises in my lifetime differently than someone of my mother's generation, and know that all problems are temporary and I will get through it. I recently read the 1995 sequel, *New Passages,* which focuses on the second half of our lives and is based on further research by Sheehy as well as her own personal experience. Again, it was insightful to me as I enter middle age. I can now look ahead to the new milestones in my life with guidance from those going before me. The book told me how rich and positive this time in our lives can be, and how many of us feel a surge in vitality and work unlike the first half of our lives. Count me in!

Louise: The Bible has always had the most impact in my life.

Louise D.: When I was forty-eight, I was required to read in a college religion studies class *Night* by Elie Wiesel. The book was terrifying. It is about a man in a concentration camp. I thought he was very courageous. He used all of his experiences to make his life better, with the hope of making a difference in someone else's life. I told my teacher that it was very hard for me to read. The book made me think

211

so hard and it hurt so much to realize what life means to someone. My teacher became teary-eyed and told me he knew it was going to be very difficult for me to read as a mother of four children. Needless to say, it was a cathartic experience.

Lynda Thomas: My favorite book is *Science and Health with Key to the Scriptures* by Mary Baker Eddy. It is my foundation for spiritual living. I also loved *All Her Paths Are Peace: Women Pioneers in Peacemaking* by Michael Henderson. The book shows the courage of many women who took the initiative to forgive and the life-changing effect it had on individuals and nations.

Lynette Horan: The *Wagons West* series by Dana Fuller Ross historically illustrates how the strength and courage of people have shaped our world through generations. I have just finished the section where birth control and a woman's right to vote became issues. It is amazing to see how far we have come. I will always appreciate the magnitude of the obstacles that held us back in those days and I recognize that they are still somewhat evident today. This helps me understand why we still have a long way to go. *The Celestine Prophecy* by James Redfield was highly recommended by my little sister (whom I adore) from my college sorority, and I am so thankful she did! This story is a mystery and an adventure in the beautiful rain forests of Peru, high in the spectacular Andes Mountains. It revolves around a search for an ancient manuscript that describes nine key insights into life. The insights lead readers on a journey to a unique spiritual awareness. The author successfully paints the word pictures of the scenery with such explicit language that you actually feel you are there. The first insight talks about the mysterious coincidences that occur in our lives and how to interpret them. WOW! This book requires intense concentration. Yet, when I was finished, I felt insightful, hopeful, and had an exciting new image of life. I frequently refer back to this book for use in my career and daily life. I just recently read and highly recommend *The Clan of the Cave Bear* and the continued *Earth Friends* series by Jean M. Auel. These books depict how an amazing and courageous woman, Ayla, loses her family in an earthquake back in the caveman era. She is hesitantly adopted by the clan—who consider her to be ugly and deformed because she is of a different kin, the kin they call "the others." This woman overcomes unbelievable obstacles (discrimination is just one) to survive with the clan and become a respected medicine woman. She is eventually cast out from the clan and required to leave her son behind. Her continued journey to find where she belongs is most admirable, illustrating courage beyond belief. She is a role model to all women.

Lynn Fullerton: The one book I have returned to over and over is *The 7 Habits of Highly Effective People* by Stephen Covey. The message that has endured with me is that as I become more independent and proactive in following my own path centered in integrity—I am able to interact with other people on the same level. While this sounds simple, the only behavior we can control is our own. The most influential habit of the seven is number five: seek first to understand, then to be understood. We generally listen to someone with the intent to reply to what they are saying—not to try to understand their point of view. In order to have the courage to be vulnerable to listen and be influenced by another, we need to be very secure within ourselves.

M. Hayes: I love C. S. Lewis's fiction *Till We Have Faces.* The book is an allegory of the two sides of ugliness and beauty. In a documentary on Lewis, they asked him what his favorite book was and he said this one. This book has spoken to me about courage and about making choices. It's all about beginning to own all of ourselves and not to lose ourselves.

Maria G.: The Bible has made a great impact on my life. I have always believed in God, but now I am starting to get into going to church again. God is always there, whether I know it or not.

Mary: Louise Hay wrote the book that made an impact in my life, *The Power Is Within You.* I was grateful to learn how to work through my emotional barriers to love myself more and to use that knowledge to encourage others to seek their own paths.

Murph Super: I loved *I Am Third* by Gale Sayers. He played football for the Chicago Bears. The title means God is first, family second, and Sayers third. These are virtues I admire in anyone. Very little of this book focuses on football. It is mostly about what Sayers goes through in life, such as losing his team buddy Brian Piccolo to cancer. He had his priorities in order. After reading the book, I realized this star player has the same emotions we all feel. My own career and place in life are just as valuable—we are all equal in our station in life.

Myrna Benoit: The one book that made the biggest impression on me was *Chicken Soup for the Soul* by Jack Canfield and Mark Victor Hansen. There is one particular story about love and the cabby, which talks about two friends. One of the men told the cabby that he was the best driver he had had that day. The friend was amazed that his friend had wasted his time and breath with the cabby. The friend said, "Why not? If I'm nice to him, he'll be nice to the next person who crosses his path." I think that's such an important message, because it doesn't hurt for us to be nice, or to be genuine. If we let that out, it will help others who in turn will help others, and maybe the world will be a better place.

Rebecca: *The Road Less Traveled* by M. Scott Peck had such a great effect on me as I read it during a time in my life when I was going through a divorce after twenty-nine years of marriage. This book was a suggestion by my psychologist. The major impact it had on me was the fact that I could have an opinion (other than my husband's) and that was not only acceptable, but definitely okay. After completing this book, I came to the realization that I held the courage to not only start over by myself, but for the first time in my life I knew in my heart that I would succeed. *Many Masters, Many Lives* by Brian Weiss made me feel as though I was coming home. Here was an extremely educated and knowledgeable person who believed and felt as I did about "old souls" and soul mates. It created a comfort level with my own spirituality. It allowed me to speak about subjects I previously felt uncomfortable discussing. I had the same exact feeling about the book *Conversations with God* by Neale Donald Walsch. The book made me feel as though someone had stepped inside my body and was speaking for me. *The Seven Laws of Spiritual Success* by Deepak Chopra was a gift to me when I arrived in Boulder. The message of the book spoke to my heart at a very vulnerable time in my life—a time when I was truly seeking direction. It gave me the courage to say "Yes" to starting over and to be positive about my future, knowing that only I, with my faith in God, held the key to my OWN success. It had proven to be a great Truth for me. Each book spoke to me at a time I was open to receiving the message within. The timing was perfect for each book—it's as though each one appeared in my life when I needed it the most.

Sarah Thompson: *The Divine Secrets of the Ya-Ya Sisterhood* by Rebecca Wells is one of those rare books that made me evaluate every part of my being. During the period I was reading it, as well as for several weeks after, I questioned, assessed, and dissected myself as a woman, as a little girl, and I think most importantly, as a friend. This book is a coming-of-age story for girls, told by the daughter of one of four girlfriends who grew up together in the 1950s. It is a magnificent tale that had the wonderful ability of making me feel like the story was being told to me but was about me. This book not only validated so many things that I thought and felt growing up, and still feel today, but made me appreciate my insecurities, laugh at my failures, and take pride in my success. Very few books have made me look at myself differently; this book did that for me. My other favorite book is the *Mists of Avalon*. Humor, battle, the doldrums of being a woman in the sixth century, and of course scandal are just a few of the reasons the *Mists of Avalon* by Marion Zimmer Bradley is at the very top of my reading list. Although many tales may have these ingredients, this book is told from the women of King Arthur's time, a time when being a woman was both physically and mentally challenging. The mysticism and honesty of these women made me proud to be female, even when Morgaine and Gwenhwyfar (the two leading ladies) act unbecoming to the sex. *Mists of Avalon* painted a picture so vivid and real; I felt as if I understood the boredom of endless days in the castle, and I delighted in the mysteries of the enchanting folds of Avalon. The women in this book made me feel confident and strong. And although I may not be a priestess in this life, after reading this book I feel certain I could pull it off in the next one.

Sally J. Kelly: I recently finished *Tuesdays with Morrie* by Mitch Albom. It is a terrific little book that had an impact on me in three ways: it touched me to realize that life is so beautiful, what is important in life, and why giving and sharing with others feeds the soul.

Sheryl Luttringer: I thoroughly enjoyed Mary Manin Morrissey's *Building Your Field of Dreams.*

This book had an impact on me because of the simple phrase "thoughts and mind reproduce after their kind." This was significant for me since I believe that we determine how our lives look, based on our thoughts and beliefs. Sometimes, when life throws us challenges, it takes courage to keep our thoughts on a positive track and prevent the negative thoughts from becoming the pattern. *Mists of Avalon* by Marion Zimmer Bradley is another book I recommend. Many women are never taught how to claim the power that is inherent in them, let alone told that it even exists. *Mists* is a wonderful reminder of the gifts we possess simply by *being* women. It's also a powerful example of what we can accomplish by being true to ourselves.

Stephie Allen: *The Story of Joan of Arc* by Albert Paine was inspiring to me as a child, to think that a teenage girl so long ago could take on the whole hierarchical system on faith alone. It set a benchmark for me, not about religion, but about courage and acting on what one thought was right and needed to be done. This book also made it very clear that it was dangerous to take on a fight. While the men may not get us on the issues, they get us nonetheless (we don't stand a chance unless we act with the support of others). It is important to keep our allies close at hand! Build our networks!

Stephanie: *Classic Christianity* by Bob George had the most impact in my life. He talks about getting right with God, which can be done once and does not have to be done daily nor every time we make a mistake. I think once we know we're right with God (forgiven, comfortable in His presence), then we can have confidence and courage throughout our life.

Sue Pierce: I enjoyed *The Aladdin Factor* by Jack Canfield and Mark Victor Hansen. The key piece of this book talks about how we never get something we don't ask for or work for. In other words, we need to ask for things—we have to go for it, such as setting goals. The courage to speak up is required to get a job we may desire. I also enjoyed *Love Must Be Tough* by James Dobson; it helped me be tough.

Ruthie: *Atlas Shrugged* by Ayn Rand, a great heroine. Her book talks a lot about societal pressures not to succeed and not to go after whatever is going to be our fulfillment. I think there are a lot of obstacles for everyone. This book is about standing on our convictions and doing it.

Theresa Hart-Kanan: When I was ten, I read *A Wrinkle in Time* by Madeleine L'Engle. This book lit up my life. I wanted to be a star traveler. I loved the characters and imagined myself being the central "girl hero" and main character, Meg Murray. She had courage, drive, compassion, and understanding beyond her years. The book was about good and evil and what happens to a world when it becomes apathetic, passive, and looks for an easy path. The book mirrored my core values and beliefs that I formulated as a child and carried into my adulthood. Today, I still believe in what Madeleine writes about. I know that one individual can make a difference. I also loved *The Little Engine That Could* by Watty Piper. As a mature woman, I still try to accomplish my goals and objectives—a commitment until the day I die. I have a clear belief system: never quit, always believe, keep going; the road has many challenges, but an individual can achieve her dreams.

Tracy: Michael Crichton's *Travels* is wonderful. He writes of his personal travels to very exclusive and sometimes treacherous areas of the world and he faces unusual experiences that take a lot of courage. Another book is *Rose Madder* by Stephen King. An odd book, it depicts a lonely, downtrodden wife who is beaten often by her policeman husband. Most of the time, these are brutal beatings. She gains the courage to leave and, throughout the book, has to face very scary situations in order to grow into a confident woman. That, to me, is courage.

Tracy Jenkins: *Beautiful Also, Are the Souls of My Black Sisters* by Dr. Jeanne Noble has had the most impact on me. Dr. Noble's book documents the extraordinary contributions made to our society by African-American women. She exploded the negative myths and stereotypes of America's Black women. This book affirmed my belief that I, too, have the attributes necessary to create opportunities for the advancement of my people. My self-confidence was bolstered by the book's empirical evidence. Moreover, the laborious challenges faced by the women taught me to have patience in my endeavors.

Virginia Heidinger: The Bible has had the most impact on me. I was inspired by *Women Who Love Too Much* by Robin Norwood. It helped me understand the relationship of a father's love for a daughter and how we end up growing up trying to please too much.

BIBLIOGRAPHY

Alcott, Louisa May. *An Old-Fashioned Girl.* Concord, Mass.: Orchard House Edition, 1936.

Aristophanes. *Lysistrata.* Translated and with introduction by Donald Sutherland. Scranton, Pa.: Chandler, 1961.

Bateson, Mary Catherine. *Composing a Life.* New York: Penguin Group, 1989.

Baum, L. Frank. *The Wonderful Wizard of Oz.* Indianapolis: Bobbs-Merrill, 1900.

Brewer, Ebenezer Cobham. *Brewer's Dictionary of Phrase and Fable.* New York: Harper Resource, 16th edition, revised by Adrian Room, 1999.

Briles, Judith. *Woman to Woman 2000: Becoming Sabotage Savvy in the New Millennium.* Far Hills, N.J.: New Horizon Press Publishers, 1999.

Brown, Rita Mae. *Rubyfruit Jungle.* New York: Bantam Books, 1973.

Condren, Mary. *The Serpent and the Goddess: Women, Religion, and Power in Celtic Ireland.* San Francisco: Harper & Row, 1989.

Covey, Stephen R. *The 7 Habits of Highly Effective People: Powerful Lessons in Personal Change*. New York: Simon & Schuster, Fireside Edition, 1989.

de Becker, Gavin. *The Gift of Fear: Survival Signals That Protect Us from Violence*. Boston: Little, Brown & Company, 1997.

Dyson, Esther. "The Sound of the Virtual Voice." *The New York Times Magazine*, May 16, 1999.

Egan, Jennifer. "Power Suffering." *The New York Times Magazine,* May 16, 1999.

Eisler, Riane Tennenhaus. *Sacred Pleasure: Sex, Myth, and the Politics of the Body*. San Francisco: Harper San Francisco, 1995.

Franklin, Benjamin. *The Autobiography of Benjamin Franklin*. New York: Macmillan Publishing Co., 1962. First Touchstone Edition, Simon & Schuster, 1997.

Gilligan, Carol. *In a Different Voice: Psychological Theory and Women's Development*. Cambridge: Harvard University Press, 1982, 1993.

Goldberger, Nancy, et al., eds. *Knowledge, Difference, and Power: Essays Inspired by Women's Ways of Knowing*. New York: Basic Books, 1996.

Goleman, Daniel. *Emotional Intelligence: Why It Can Matter More Than IQ*. New York: Bantam Books, 1994.

Hargrove, Robert. *Masterful Coaching: Extraordinary Results by Impacting People and the Way They Think and Work Together.* San Francisco: Jossey-Bass Pfeiffer, 1995.

Jaworski, Joseph. *Synchronicity: The Inner Path of Leadership.* San Francisco: Berrett-Koehler Publishers, 1996.

McCorduck, Pamela, and Nancy Ramsey (contributor). *The Futures of Women.* Reading, Mass.: Addison-Wesley Publishing Company, 1996.

MacIntyre, Alasdair. *After Virtue: A Study in Moral Theory.* American Edition. South Bend, Ind.: University of Notre Dame Press, 1981.

Maturana, H., and F. Varela. *The Tree of Knowledge: The Biological Roots of Human Understanding.* Boston: Shambhala Publications, 1987, 1991.

Meter, Van Jonathan. "Oprah's Moment." *Vogue,* October 1998.

Minard, Rosemary, ed. *Womenfolk and Fairy Tales.* Boston: Houghton Mifflin Company, 1975.

Morgan, Susan. "Par Excellence." *Mirabella,* March 1999.

Myss, Caroline, Ph.D. *Anatomy of the Spirit: The Seven Stages of Power and Healing.* New York: Harmony Books, 1996.

Nix, William H. *Character Works*. Nashville: Broadman & Holman, 1999.

Palmer, Helen. *The Enneagram in Love and Work: Understanding Your Intimate and Business Relationships*. San Francisco: Harper San Francisco, 1995.

Pearman, Roger R., and Sarah C. Albritton. *I'm Not Crazy, I'm Just Not You: The Real Meaning of the 16 Personality Types*. Palo Alto, Calif.: Davis-Black Publishing, 1997.

Pearson, Carol S. *The Hero Within: Six Archetypes We Live By*. New York: HarperCollins, 1986.

Pierre, Peggy Claude. "Anorexia: A Tale of Two Daughters." *Vogue*, September 1997.

Pipher, Mary. *Reviving Ophelia: Saving the Selves of Adolescent Girls*. New York: Putnam Publishing Group, 1994.

Robbins, Michael. *Tapestry of the Gods, Section One*. Mariposa, Calif.: University of the Seven Rays Publishing House, 1996.

Shakespeare, William. *Cymbeline*. Edited by M. R. Ridley. London: Dent; New York: Dutton, 1935.

Shlain, Leonard. *The Alphabet Versus the Goddess: The Conflict Between Word and Image*. New York: Penguin Group–Viking, 1998.

Sontag, Susan. "Women." *Vogue*, November 1999.

Stoddard, Alexandra. *Making Choices: Discover the Joy in Living the Life You Want to Lead.* New York: Avon Books, 1994.

Stone, Merlin. *When God Was a Woman.* Great Britain: Harvest/HBJ edition, Dial Press, 1976.

Tarule, Mattuck Jill. "Voices in Dialogue: Collaborative Ways of Knowing." In *Knowledge, Difference, and Power: Essays Inspired by Women's Ways of Knowing.* Edited by Goldberger et al. New York: Basic Books, 1996.

Terwilliger, Cate. "Battle On!" *Denver Post,* September 14, 1998 (Scene section).

Wells, Diana. *100 Flowers and How They Got Their Names.* Chapel Hill: Algonquin Books of Chapel Hill, 1997.

Wolf, Naomi. "The Future Is Ours to Lose." *The New York Times Magazine,* May 16, 1999.

The Wizard of Oz (film). Victor Fleming, director. Hollywood: Metro-Goldwyn-Mayer Pictures, 1939. Based on L. Frank Baum's *The Wonderful Wizard of Oz,* 1900.

INDEX

AUTHOR'S NOTE

*I feel there is something unexplored about women
that only a woman can explore . . .*

Georgia O'Keeffe

All of the life histories included in this book are the
true and actual experiences of the women interviewed. Because some of the women did not want
their names revealed, I have used only first names
throughout the book. In a few instances even the
first names have been changed to protect identities,
but their stories are exactly as told to me.

I am most grateful to all of the women who
shared their life experiences, their precious time,
their pain. Their courageous spirits are an inspiration to women everywhere. I thank them with all
my heart. I also thank all of the medical, sociologi-
cal, theological, and psychological professionals
with whom I consulted about the premise of this
book, the authors quoted, and the friends who encouraged and consoled me during the long months
of preparing the manuscript.

Sandra Ford Walston
Denver, Colorado
January 2000

ABOUT THE AUTHOR

Sandra Ford Walston is intimately familiar with the power of courage. A devout Catholic, she became pregnant at age twenty while attending college by someone she did not want to marry and endured a lonely and frightening pregnancy. In a dark confessional she rediscovered her "courageous will" and made a decision to place her son in a loving family. This decision profoundly affected the rest of her life.

In 1990, after enjoying successful careers in banking, real estate, and education, she started a private consulting practice to design, develop, and conduct interpersonal-skills seminars for adults. A professional speaker and trainer, an executive coach, and a facilitator of retreats for corporate boards and shareholders, she also provides courage coaching for individuals, specializing in courage for women.

From 1984 to the present, Sandra Walston has taught business seminars at UCLA, Colorado State University, University of Denver, and the Colorado Society of Certified Public Accountants. She has published numerous articles (see Website below) and designed more than fifty interpersonal-skills training programs. She conducts programs for public and private businesses to surmount challenges in the following areas: team building, communication, change, leadership, "managing up," sales, customer service, time management, gaining group consensus, and developing camaraderie and trust. Her passion is to help individuals and groups discover their hidden talents.

Ms. Walston is qualified to administer and interpret the Myers-Briggs Type Indicator® and she is certified in the Enneagram.

Visit her Website at www.walstoncourage.com for more information or to order books.